I0040086

Growing Your Business

Growing Your Business

Sanjyot P. Dunung

business**expert**
Press

Growing Your Business

Copyright © Sanjyot P. Dunung, 2010
All rights reserved. No part of this publication may be reproduced, stored in a retrieval system, or transmitted in any form or by any means—electronic, mechanical, photocopy, recording, or any other except for brief quotations, not to exceed 400 words, without the prior permission of the publisher.

First published in 2010 by
Business Expert Press, LLC
222 East 46th Street, New York, NY 10017
www.businessexpertpress.com

ISBN-13: 978-1-60649-133-1 (paperback)
ISBN-10: 1-60649-133-4 (paperback)

ISBN-13: 978-1-60649-132-4 (e-book)
ISBN-10: 1-60649-132-6 (e-book)

10.4128/9781606491324

A publication in the Business Expert Press Small Business Management and Entrepreneurship collection

Collection ISSN: 1946-5653 (print)
Collection ISSN: 1946-5661 (electronic)

Cover design by Jonathan Pennell
Interior design by Scribe, Inc.

First edition: May 2010

10 9 8 7 6 5 4 3 2 1

Printed in the United States of America.

To Shanth, Yash, and Anand:

Find your own special star and reach for it.
Follow your hearts and true passions.

To my fellow entrepreneurs:

"Do not go where the path may lead, go instead where there is no path and leave a trail."

—Ralph Waldo Emerson

Abstract

In the hard-fought business world, only one new business in 20 lives to see its fifth anniversary. Typical management books do not address the unique nuances of early-stage companies. Most entrepreneurial books often profile successful entrepreneurs or companies who are better known, which usually includes only the small percentage that achieve stratospheric success. *Growing Your Own Business* shares the secrets of long-term survival and success, detailing practical guidelines, and relevant "tales from the trenches" to help entrepreneurs tackle common concerns and obstacles. A welcome combination of first-person how-to advice and peer mentoring support, this comprehensive, essential resource book provides sound, battle-proven advice for developing effective sales and marketing strategies, managing employees, and navigating business cycles. *Growing Your Own Business* continues after the first book, *Starting Your Own Business*. This resource is designed to work as independent resource or integrate into business curriculums.

Keywords

Entrepreneurship, guerilla marketing, small business, managing a business, governance, small business cycles

Contents

Acknowledgments

Books like *Growing Your Business* come from years of collective experiences and discussions. There are many, many people whose wise counsel and insight I have benefited from and who have directly and indirectly contributed to this book. I am grateful to all of these people who have through the years touched my life and my businesses.

I also want to express my sincere gratitude to the people who worked for, worked with, advised, or invested in my companies. The concept for this book came as I navigated the entrepreneurial opportunities, bumps, and challenges. Over the years, many of you also experienced the same entrepreneurial cycles with me and generously shared your insight, wisdom, enthusiasm, professionalism, and above all, friendship. Thank you.

This book would not have emerged in its current form if it weren't for the inspiration and input of some wonderful fellow entrepreneurs and friends. Their stories bring to life much of the lessons of *Growing Your Business* and follow in the pages hereafter. All of their personal experiences, attitudes, passions, and enthusiasm highlight what attracts so many to the intriguing world of entrepreneurship. All of you have been instrumental as I navigated the gray, fuzzy space between professional and personal worlds that each of us must come to terms with at various junctures in our lives.

To my wonderful boys, Shanth, Yash, and Anand, thank you for your patience in letting me spend the weekends needed to finish this book. Your contagious giggles, hugs, and antics provided inspiration and clarity at just the right times. To my parents, a most heartfelt thank you for always being there when it was needed most and embodying the lifelong values of hard work, passion, kindness, integrity, discipline, and generosity of heart and spirit. For many decades, you have both lived exemplary lives and you continue to do so.

Author's Note

There are a lot of experiences, stories, facts, and opinions in this book. I'd like to clearly state that the opinions in this book, if not directly attributed to a fellow entrepreneur, are mine or as a direct result of research I've conducted. I bear full responsibility for any inaccuracies and/or omissions of all that follows in the pages ahead.

I hope that this book provides you with insight and essential information on your own entrepreneurial journey. I'd love to hear from fellow entrepreneurs and those who work in the worlds of entrepreneurship, including employees, VCs, investors, advisors, and customers. If you'd like to submit a potential "Tales from the Trenches" for the next edition or just have an interesting or really great personal story, please send it to me at spdunung@msn.com. Please note that while I can't acknowledge receipt for all stories, no experiences will be used without the sender's final permission.

Thank you for making this book part of your entrepreneurial journey! I hope it provides you the necessary insight as you commence or continue to navigate the entrepreneurial peaks, valleys, and bumps.

Introduction

Like many entrepreneurs, when I started my first company, I didn't know any other entrepreneurs. My frame of reference was the corporate world, in which I had cut my professional teeth, so to speak. As I progressed, I found myself facing all sorts of opportunities and challenges that I would have been able to navigate much more smoothly had I had the knowledge I do now. It was not until I was well into operating my second company that I began to meet fellow entrepreneurs whose companies were at similar stages of growth. Once we began to share experiences, I realized that I was not alone and that my experiences were not unique.

One of the most difficult challenges entrepreneurs encounter is the feeling of aloneness when facing all the business issues of starting, growing, and running their own company. The reality is that while many of the challenges that entrepreneurs face are unique to entrepreneurship, individual entrepreneurs are certainly not alone. Many entrepreneurs feel as though no one else has made a certain mistake or faced a particular challenge, when in truth, many have.

After many coffees and cocktails with fellow entrepreneurs, I realized that there were no sources any of us could turn to to read about "real-life" experiences. All the books on entrepreneurship were written by journalists or consultants and lacked a real understanding of what it was like to be "in the trenches."

Also, most entrepreneurial books profile only enormously successful entrepreneurs or companies, thereby bypassing much of the common entrepreneurial experience. Not every company can be a Dell or Microsoft, yet thousands of entrepreneurs happily achieve a high level of success far beyond the sole proprietorship stage. My focus is on the millions of entrepreneurs looking to find success in this range.

As entertaining and inspiring as the rags-to-riches stories may be, it is important to focus on the opportunities, challenges, mistakes, and bumps in the road. It's important to know what the start-up and early years of highly successful companies were really like on a day-to-day basis. There's a prevalence of public relations–generated images of young entrepreneurs in garages or dorm rooms, which then fast-forward to a very successful post-IPO (initial public offering) world. The decade or more in between is a vague blur and rarely referenced, yet every company and entrepreneur faces many of the same challenges during those growth years. Even the most successful entrepreneur experiences bumps in the road and may need to fold several companies before finding the right "recipe" for success.

Further, the reality is that most entrepreneurs have no guarantee of success. Clearly, you feel optimistic about your possibilities or you wouldn't be engaged in your current project. However, you can't know for sure. You just believe and hope that you're right. Michael Dell and Bill Gates didn't wake up one morning in their early years and know for sure that they would create multibillion dollar companies within one or two decades. Few focus on the fact that it's passion, not a clairvoyant guarantee of success, that fuels the entrepreneur on a daily basis.

This is the handbook I wish I'd had when I began my first business. In it, I've tried to incorporate all the knowledge I gleaned from having had several businesses. Often, the most frustrating quandary for entrepreneurs, and for people in general, is that they don't know what questions to ask early on, because they don't know what they don't know.

In this book, I've tried to highlight the range of key issues that you need to consider every step of the way. Of course, we have all had a little entrepreneurial optimistic arrogance at one point or another and thought we could handle everything just fine. As we get more seasoned, we realize that while that may be true in some situations, it would be much less stressful to be able to anticipate and be prepared for opportunities, challenges, and bumps in the road.

Entrepreneurship is a spiritual journey where you learn as much about yourself as you do about your business, products, and customers. What I hope will make this book useful is that it provides relevant facts while nourishing the entrepreneur's spiritual journey.

Those who think entrepreneurship is just hard facts, business, and dollars and cents have probably never met a real entrepreneur. I am not just talking about the human side of a company and the problems it can cause—something all organizations encounter. I am referring to the intense soul-searching an entrepreneur goes through when asking himself or herself a slew of questions every day while encountering opportunities and obstacles. It's about the passion and believing all the way deep into your gut and soul. For that reason, you'll find that I'll talk at times about the things you'll need to reflect on at different stages of the start-up phase.

I was moved to write this book because of my personal experiences. I'm on my third company as a career entrepreneur. Through all three I've made a good number of mistakes and many smart moves, some as a result of careful planning and strategy and others from luck and timing. Entrepreneurship encompasses all of it—the successes, challenges, mistakes, and comebacks. I wanted to write a book for novices as well as for seasoned career entrepreneurs, for companies with revenues of six figures as well as companies of nine figures. I've also written this book for potential entrepreneurs, for people thinking of starting their own companies, to help them understand what they may encounter along the way. I have personally ridden the entrepreneurial roller coaster, and it's a great ride for those who are ready for it.

My entrepreneurial experience started quite early in my life. Even as a child, I was always starting a business of some sort. As I was not content to have just another lemonade stand, my "business" was a successful little Sunday-morning camp for neighborhood kids. I charged a mere 50 cents per child for 2 hours—quite a bargain in today's terms—and I soon realized I had much to learn about pricing. It was the first of many ideas, and I gradually learned, as many entrepreneurs do, that it's a long way from a great idea to tangible success.

My first company sort of fell into my lap, which is how many entrepreneurs find their first firm. In my case, my first company was offered to me by a friend who wanted to move to the new Czech Republic and needed to "sell" her business, which was in essence one client. I jumped at the opportunity. I bought the "business" and her fax machine for $500. The client didn't make much money, and sales were very low by my heady expectations. I knew I needed to expand and again "the entrepreneurial opportunity" found me. It was the early 1990s and Asia was starting to boom. Sensing the opportunity, I expanded into providing companies with cultural training services and products to enter and operate in the

Asian market. At the same time, we helped Asian companies learn about and enter the American market.

We grew quickly until the Asian economic crisis of 1997 started to unravel our key overseas partners and our sales plateaued. I then realized, along with some key customers, that taking our training methodology, materials, and know-how to a technology platform would be highly beneficial for them and profitable for us. It was the beginning of the dot-com period, and although we weren't a dot-com, we certainly rode the early wave.

By this point, after a decade plus in the "culture" business, I was deeply passionate about the need for great products to help people of all ages learn about different cultures. I had always wanted to run my own firm, and I wanted to grow one from a unique idea or vision that I knew was germinating deep within. This was an approach that worked well for me. I had discovered a market need, developed ideas, and because of this, my life's passion was born.

Despite my enthusiasm and the advantage of external funding, my second company was a bit ahead of its time and fell victim to the post-9/11 economic collapse and a disincentivizing capital structure. It's taken me until my third company to get the right formula and timing to create a growing and profitable education company. Through it all, my vision has stayed fairly consistent, only evolving with market opportunity and demand. This has enabled me to continue building my knowledge, network, and experience.

Many people are surprised to learn that successful entrepreneurs do not always have a perfect business plan and marketing and sales strategy in place before launching their businesses. In fact, many often deviate so significantly from the original plan that the business is unrecognizable. Instead, what seems to be the mark of a successful entrepreneur is the ability to adeptly navigate the daily, weekly, and monthly bumps, twists, and turns in the life of a young or small company.

We live in a world of instant gratification. People want instant success along with everything else. There are no prepackaged sure paths to successful entrepreneurship. You'll notice from the title that this book does not promise a get-rich-quick scheme. This book is about building growing, sustainable businesses and the experiences that most entrepreneurs go through.

I'll relay one of the more sound pieces of advice I have received—start a business for what you can get out of it this year, not 3 to 5 years down the road—because you're not likely to make it to that future point if you can't take care of today. Pay yourself a salary and strive for profitability.

If you're looking for a how-to book with a step-by-step outline for guaranteed success, don't look here. You won't find that in this book. In fact, you won't find it anywhere, and you should be wary of those who promise such formulaic approaches. There is no guaranteed formula for success. The path to successful entrepreneurship is unique in every circumstance. The product, the market, and the timing are all unique. Something that works in one mix may not work in another. What's similar is the *spirit* that bonds entrepreneurs.

I'm not going to suggest that I have all the answers and have figured out this entrepreneurship thing to a science. What makes a successful entrepreneur is 50% ingenuity, 50% luck and timing, and 100% hard work. If you're quickly doing the math and ready to write to my editors about a typo, it's intentional. Entrepreneurship is not an exact science, it's an art. I've often heard that luck is defined as preparedness meets opportunity.

Growing a successful business requires vision and passion. Some have tried to make it a science, hence the preponderance of venture capital (VC) incubators, which are insulated breeding labs for taking an idea and hiring a management team to take the idea and make it an enduring and growing company. The reality is that these incubators have produced limited success. They're missing the key ingredient, the zealous entrepreneur, who's convinced that his or her idea *is* the next best thing to sliced bread and is ready to go for broke—in some cases literally. Cherry picking a bunch of successful professionals and asking them to launch a new venture is like a soda without the fizz. It's missing the key ingredient—the entrepreneur's passion. It's the passion that helps the entrepreneur keep the faith during the start-up and the growth phases as well as the difficult times and eventually successfully navigate the entrepreneurial opportunities and bumps along the way.

When I decided to write this book, I had some initial qualms. To be of value, this book needed to be honest, which meant the necessity of admitting and publicly analyzing both my successes and my failures. The

Japanese have a cultural concept called *honne* versus *tatemae*, which means *real* truth as opposed to the "public" truth. I realized that as entrepreneurs we needed a *honne* book; in other words, a real truth book. We want to know what it's really like to experience the stages of starting and growing a young company, from developing sales and marketing strategies to managing product, employee, and finance issues, to keeping the faith during the good and bad times.

When I speak on entrepreneurship, I often find that audiences are more interested in the challenges, pitfalls, problems, and failures. The successes are of course very important, but everyone is willing to share those. What's lacking is a candid discussion of entrepreneurship by entrepreneurs. We often learn more about business not through the successes, but through the analysis and soul-searching of failures.

Seasoned entrepreneurs will also find great value in this book. The presented situations and experiences are real, and most people can relate to the challenges and opportunities. First time entrepreneurs will certainly find value as well, but the experiences presented in this book will ring a bit more true after you've started down the entrepreneurial road. In this book you'll find real life experiences from entrepreneurs and myself. These "tales from the trenches" help to illustrate a point in the relevant chapter.

I can't, despite my best intentions, reduce entrepreneurship to 10 easy steps as if there were some mechanical formula. Life should be so easy. We'd have a heck of lot more successful entrepreneurs. This is more about what to look for along the way. No one can predict his or her path with any surety; all you can do is prepare for the range of "wild animals" and "weather conditions." Pursuing entrepreneurship needn't be difficult, but you need to understand that it's also not formulaic. There is no perfect business plan, no perfect amount of start-up funding, no perfect organizational structure, and so on. Rather, it's a combination of what works for you. Growing a successful company requires that you manage a slew of issues simultaneously, often with inadequate resources and information. As you navigate the world of entrepreneurship, this handbook will provide you with the range of options, experiences, and strategies to help you successfully grow your company.

CHAPTER 1

Marketing and Sales

Marketing and sales are the life source of your company. You can make the best product or provide the optimal service, but it's irrelevant if you can't sell or your customer won't buy. Like business plans, marketing plans evolve with an organization. In this chapter, I'll review the core components of marketing and sales and give you things to think about as your company grows.

Marketing and sales are often mistakenly considered one and the same, even at the largest and oldest of companies. Marketing designs strategy and sales implements, but in reality, salespeople gather very valuable information that helps fine-tune the strategy, forming a delicate balance between the two departments. In many organizations, there's a struggle between marketing and sales as to which directs which. If you work to coordinate these areas in a complementary way, you're likely to have a more successful strategy, and more importantly, you'll be able to adjust your strategy quickly in response to market conditions.

Many entrepreneurs are actually quite good at some aspects of marketing and sales, usually as early promoters of the venture, as it takes a bit of sales to get a company off the ground. It's the sales vocabulary that sometimes confuses people. As with most industries, the marketing, sales, and advertising world has its own lingo. Don't let the lingo trip you up. Focus instead on the concepts' objectives.

Many companies err because they don't fine-tune their marketing strategy enough. Plan to visit your strategy at least quarterly. Monitor sales, customer feedback, and industry trends. If you do this frequently enough, you're less likely to be surprised by any industry changes and more likely to be able to incorporate new information steadily.

Integrated Growth Strategies

Before you develop your marketing and sales plan, you need to be sure there really is a market for what you are making and selling. Companies of all sizes routinely forget to verify the market before they launch marketing campaigns. When sales are below expectations, they reassess the plan, not whether their product or service actually has a market. Once you have market verification, you can begin to develop an appropriate marketing and sales plan.

The most fundamental question to answer is "What problem am I solving with this service/product?" If you cannot answer that question in a way that compels customers to say "I'll buy it," friends to say "cool," or investors to say "tell me more," then perhaps rethinking the concept is in order.

Assuming you have studied the opportunity and believe you have something unique, market size becomes another consideration. Are there enough buyers in your market? How big is your industry category, and how much potential overall money is available to buy products or services like yours? If you're offering a very niche product, you may need to take into account that you will only be able to grow to a certain size, even if all the stars and moons line up.

Market Research

Today, the Internet provides a rich and free source of market research. It should be one of the first places you go to find industry data, competitive information, corporate name availability, and marketing opportunities such as trade show listings.

An essential part of any marketing or sales plan is the research phase. A lot of entrepreneurs use the media to follow trends. The media can be a useful source—to an extent. Don't let your use of the media replace more specialized research. Try to find out as much as possible about the writer or lead researcher. Most are professional writers and might not necessarily have enough experience in your industry to interpret market-specific information accurately. Further, there are very few writers or reporters who have formal business training or experience. This doesn't mean that you should dismiss traditional business publications and newspapers, but rather that you should utilize the facts to make your own conclusions rather than blindly adopt the reasoning of the published word.

Gathering information from these types of sources is called secondary research. It's critical to take the time to find out about the competitive landscape and market potential before spending a lot of time, energy, and money chasing the wrong idea. You can access a wide base of resources, publications, and potential customers. Verify and evaluate the credibility of lesser-known sources. Otherwise, you may get incorrect information. It helps if you can verify information obtained online with an off-line source, such as an industry expert.

Despite the utility of secondary research, you will still need primary research to help build out your offering and to set the course for how you're going to market your product. Primary research's fundamental role is to provide feedback specific to your product or service. It can be as informal as interviewing people familiar with the industry or as formal as hiring a professional research firm to conduct sophisticated studies with quantifiable results.

More structured interviews with potential customers can also be useful. It's amazing how many companies do not take this critical step. Understanding the pain, buying preference, and motivational behavior of this audience makes all the difference in knowing whether your product meets their needs.

Companies that need direct customer input find focus groups useful. Utilizing focus groups is part of an overall marketing strategy, and you need to be clear on the profile of the participants as well as the objectives for each group. You should use experienced focus group leaders to facilitate these meetings.

Developing a Marketing and Sales Plan

Going through the marketing and sales planning process enables you to focus on how you'll reach your customer and complete the sale. If appropriate, you'll be able to prepare for a repeat sale—preparation that is critical for ongoing sustainability.

The plan is simply the document that will state the strategy and allow you to track it. In the business plan, you'll include macro-level parts of your marketing and sales strategy. In the marketing plan, you add the details. Both marketing and sales have several key factors to focus on. We'll start by looking at marketing first.

Marketing

There are several key areas that you'll need to focus on as you plan your marketing strategy:

- Product or service
- Target market
- Pricing
- Distribution
- Building a brand
- Advertising and promotions

Product or Service

Your business plan will include an in-depth description of your product or service. Use your marketing plan to expand the description to include uniqueness, service options, warranties, and other features and benefits. By understanding your core target market, you'll be able to refine your description even further.

What's Your Unique Selling Position?

It's essential to have a unique selling position (USP). For some companies, it's the uniqueness of their product. For others, it's their low price, and for others, it might be their distribution. By distribution, I am referring to how a customer can obtain the product or service. Where or how can they buy it? Is it exclusively or readily available? Often a USP is a combination of factors, as markets do not remain static but are constantly changing. A product that is new and unique today may have many competitors within 6 to 24 months, especially if it's successful. Its USP may initially be that it is new and unique. Over time, the USP may evolve to be new product versions or price or both.

The importance of articulating a USP *cannot* be understated. It is *the* most important sentence you say about your company. Some call it the "elevator pitch," based on the concept that if someone on an elevator asks you what your company does, you have only the time between the tenth floor and ground floor to say something compelling, so that by the time you get off, the rider is saying "tell me more."

Putting your pitch down on paper is critical to the process of developing a compelling USP. Your pitch should be no more than two sentences and should capture the imagination of the listener while explaining the need you are meeting in your particular market. Working with your team on this can be a very enlightening experience. Don't be surprised to find it a very difficult task. However, once you have reached consensus, you'll find you've created a clear vision for the company that others can now execute.

Features and Benefits

You'll need to be clear not only about how your product will work or how a service will be delivered, but if you intend to provide additional features and benefits. There's an added cost to such things as providing warranties and customer service, and you'll need to account for those in your budget.

You'll also need to think about when you need to have a new product version, based on industry standards. Your product or service will continue to evolve over time, particularly as you respond to competitive pressures and market demand. You may offer new features or service features, like warranties and customer support. All of these help determine the value for your product or service.

If your core offering is based on price value, you need to be confident that your competitors can't (not just won't, but actually *can't*) match you while you grow to critical mass. Your competitors won't be able to match you if you have a new technology that allows you to build more cheaply. You need to plan for how much time it will take to build that critical market share. You're best off if you can add to the lowest cost feature by adding a nonmonetary value such as a service feature.

Target Market

Knowing your target market is critical. Many businesspeople confuse buyers with users and market to the user and not the buyer. Who is your customer and who's your user? In some cases, they are one and the same, but other times they're different. You'll need to know the demographics of both of them.

Understand how your buyers decide to "buy." What influences their decision? Are they motivated by low cost, high quality, easy access, or the prestige of a brand? Often, they are motivated by a combination of these factors. It's important to monitor all these influences, because they are likely to change over time in order of importance.

Talk to your customer and your potential customer as early as you can. Create informal focus groups to test and use your products. If you can, reach out to potential competitors, partners, industry experts, and so on. Their input is essential in growing a company. It's also helpful to talk to potential advisors and even venture capitalists (VCs), as everyone has a piece of wisdom to share, much of which could be quite valuable.

Trade Shows

A trade show offers a great opportunity to learn more about your target market as well as the market in general. You'll be able to see how your likely competition "speaks" to your target customer. You can also learn a great deal about the nuances of the industry. You do not need to exhibit to attend a trade show. Many offer a day's pass for a fee and occasionally require some proof of industry activity. In many cases, that proof is as simple as a business card with the company name, address, and Web site.

Industry association Web sites are a great way to find potential competitors. Lists of trade show exhibitors can also direct you to the same type of information.

In these days of trade show overkill, the best way to find the most productive trade shows is to find out which ones competitors and customers attend. One or two key shows are all that you need. You can search online by your market or industry association. You can also find trade shows by searching on the Web site of your city's or another major city's convention center. The bigger the trade show, the more expansive its range of exhibitors and customers. However, keep in mind that trade shows are an industry and business in themselves. Be wary of hard sells to exhibit or attend.

Many trade shows also provide a forum for continuing education or training for professionals. If you're looking to influence doctors, then attending a conference or trade show on medicine will likely put you near your target market. If you're interested in selling companywide solutions, you need to be sure that decision makers attend the show and not just junior staff who may be doing course work.

Price

Pricing your product or service is always tricky. If you have established competitors, then there are some industry benchmarks. But your USP may suggest that there is the opportunity to challenge the industry pricing, either at higher or lower levels. Make sure to account for customer service and related expenses when determining your price. Many entrepreneurs don't realize the cost of these features and then are faced with cash flow challenges.

There are many books and articles on how to approach pricing—some theoretical and some practical. While pricing is industry and market specific, there are two basic ways to approach pricing. You may want to read a marketing reference book or access resources, particularly if you don't have a business background. Business educations, no matter how stellar, are rarely enough to navigate the world of entrepreneurship—you need the real-world experience to completely understand how to apply your education.

The first pricing approach is based on cost plus a margin. This basically determines your cost per unit and then adds a margin that is appropriate for your industry. Obviously, you want to maximize sales revenue, but you should focus on profitability or margins, which refers to the revenues or sales minus the actual or direct cost of making your product or providing your service. For your reference, indirect costs are all the expenses you incur that are not directly related to actually making the product or providing the service. Indirect expenses include all overhead costs such as office rent, office administrative costs, and professional expenses for lawyers and accountants.

The risk for new companies in using cost-based pricing is underestimating their costs. Just about *all* entrepreneurial ventures underestimate their costs. Even the most established and largest companies routinely under budget for product development. One option is to provide a margin for unanticipated costs, but realistically, your figures may not take everything into account. It's not uncommon to be over budget by more than 50%.

The second approach prices according to what the market will pay for your product or service. Take a look at competitors' pricing. If you believe that your product's USP puts it in a new pricing category, take a look at some possible comparables and estimate what mark up you think the market will pay for the unique new features.

The first step in the market-based pricing approach is to make sure you can profitably make the product for that price. You need to not just break even, but to be *profitable* with a clear and healthy margin. This is where it's important to understand industry benchmarks. Some industries have margins less than 50% and others have margins around 90%. Larger margins provide more room for indirect costs and a solid net income. Service-related businesses where labor costs are high tend to have lower margins.

Your customers will not pay more for a product or service unless they clearly understand the perceived benefit or extra feature. Also, pricing yourself too far below the market may call into question issues of quality or service. If a lower price is part of your USP, you need to clearly communicate that in your marketing efforts. When you do your budgeting, look at your margins to make sure they are competitive with your industry. Your long-term viability depends on this factor, especially if your competitors are more profitable and will have more to invest in marketing or product development.

If your product or service is completely new to market, you may want to look at similar products or services, although not necessarily competitors. For example, for a new drink with no perceived direct competitors, you will do well to research pricing and margins of other soft drinks and fruit drinks. You may be able to charge more, as Starbucks has demonstrated, but your customer must clearly understand and value the perceived features and benefits. In Starbucks' case, the taste and variety of the coffee, along with the comfortable ambiance, allowed the company to charge more for a cup of coffee and led the company to success.

In practice, most companies will use both approaches, cost plus a margin and market-based pricing, to come up with one or more price points. You can then use industry benchmarks and market feedback to finalize the price. Always aim for the highest price the market can bear. It's relatively easier to lower your price than to increase it for the same product or service. Companies that are able to increase their pricing beyond the basic inflation percentages usually have to offer new features or benefits. You don't usually have to justify a price decrease.

Some companies also conduct price tests before finalizing a particular price. You may want to use this option if the industry benchmarks and market demand are not clear. You can do a "limited run" and offer your product at select price points. You can even try different price points to test small market samples. This test-pricing approach has been used successfully for products offered through catalogs or direct mail. Companies print limited catalogs or direct mailers with different prices and mail them to different target audiences. This method is increasingly less common as a result of the Internet, where it's much harder to control which target audiences have access to which price points.

If you decide to test pricing, have a clear strategy in place and be in direct communication with your customers. This is, of course, easier to do with smaller groups of customers. Sales may vary for a variety of reasons aside from pricing, and you need to be in touch with your customers to understand what is impacting their buying decisions.

For service firms or custom projects, many firms use a cost multiple to determine the price they should charge a customer. To obtain the multiple, companies look at the indirect costs and spread them over the projected revenues for the year. Many firms use cost multiples of between two and three times.

For example, if a project will cost $1,000 in direct costs, most likely labor related, it would be multiplied by a cost factor of, say, 2.5 to determine the final fee that the customer should be charged; $2,500 in this case. The cost multiple ensures that the indirect costs are spread over all the projects. Some service industries can get away with higher multiples by increasing the gross margin. If you're faced with lower multiples, you may want to assess the pricing and analyze your venture and the industry overall, as you're in a low-margin business.

Distribution

Determining the optimal distribution strategy will help you determine your sales strategy. Will you sell to your customer directly or through resellers or both? Learning what is typical for your industry will help you understand your customers' expectations. You don't want to spend unnecessary and extra marketing expense to educate your customers on how to find your products or service if they already know where to look for your competitors.

You may also have more than one market for your product or service, and each market may be accessed by a different distribution channel. For example, you may sell through retail stores as well as through value-added resellers who will sell your products along with their other products.

How your customers obtain your product or service is a critical issue. You can have a great product, but if your customers can't find it or you can't get it in front of your customers, there's no sale. This is particularly relevant in the retail industry. Retail distribution is challenging because shelf space is often controlled by large companies. In the retail world, you're "selling and marketing" to the distributor, retail buyer, or both as well as to your end user and store customers. Communicating with all these groups may require several different communication strategies. You'll need to determine how best to forge essential partnerships.

For example, let's say that you have a great new take on an old classic: chocolate chip cookies. Your product's USP is that it's chewier and tastier than other store-bought cookies. You'd love to be on the shelves of giant national supermarkets like those found in Wal-Mart, but those shelves are often controlled by large product companies, many of which are likely to see you as a tiny competitor. It could take quite a while to get on the shelves of Wal-Mart or a major grocery chain. Your better option in the early stages of your company may be to focus on gourmet food stores, where new, high-quality products may find earlier and easier reception from both the store and customers.

Companies also consider direct mail or catalogs. Both options have been successful and there are pros and cons to each. More recently, the Internet enabled many companies to reach potential customers directly. In each of these three options there is a cost to acquiring each customer. "Acquisition cost" refers to the money it takes to get each customer. It includes purchasing names from a database, mailing costs if it's direct mail or catalog, and Web advertising or similar promotional costs. You'll need to assess these costs as you evaluate the optimal distribution channels.

Remember that each channel does have a cost, even if it may not be readily evident. For example, if you act as a wholesaler and sell to resellers or buyers, your costs will include sales support staff, marketing materials, and trade shows. We'll cover developing sales teams later in this chapter.

Some businesses sell into channels at a low margin because the volume of their sale compensates for the margin or because the exposure enhances their overall brand. This is often the case for product companies that sell through Wal-Mart. The mass retailer has a reputation and history of squeezing manufacturers' margins. Some have even claimed that they sell at a loss in this channel. However, for most, the benefit is clear. The potential volume is one of the largest and provides exposure to the widest customer base. This is an example of the types of pros and cons of pricing in different channels that you'll need to review. There is no correct way to arrive at a price for your product. The strategy you decide to employ depends on your company, the stage of your company, and your overall marketing and sales strategy.

Building a Brand

Many people share the misconception that a brand is a company's logo. While the logo is a visual "expression" of the brand, it is not *the* brand.

A brand is the entire package. It is everything about your company. It is how people perceive your offering and the experience they would have if they should choose to select your product or service.

If you are Apple, your brand represents youthful, cool, and cutting-edge technologies and consumer electronics products. And yes, the Apple logo reflects that image as well. If you are Starbucks, your brand represents community, comfort, and enlightenment while enjoying unusual (and expensive) coffee or tea drinks.

On the other hand, if you are the *Wall Street Journal*, you are serious, astute, and rich with knowledge, connections, and quality business news coverage. You are *the* source for savvy business people who want to be "in the know" about important business events and experiences.

One of the first exercises a good marketing firm should do is help you define your brand personality. This definition should then drive how you market yourself, how you create your business environment, the kinds of personalities you hire, and the way you interact with your customers and partners.

One of the first expressions you'll develop from this base is your corporate name and logo. Think about what would have happened if Google had named itself Knowledge Vault. The name Knowledge Vault conveys a very different feeling, doesn't it? Next imagine how the logo would have looked if it was designed around the name and brand personality of Knowledge Vault. Of course, the name Knowledge Vault conveys the company's purpose a lot faster than the name Google. Remember that anytime you do something different and bold like this, you must be prepared to invest heavily in its initial marketing.

Advertising and Promotion

There are many ways to promote your company and products. To decide which medium is best, talk with your market and find out how your potential customers tend to receive information. Do they read magazines? If so, which ones? Do they use the Web to find resources?

What sites do they like? Do they go to trade shows? Which ones? Is direct mail or telemarketing more effective?

Determining the best course of promotional investment will depend on many variables such as the following:

- Is this a business-to-consumer offering or a business-to-business offering?
- How big is the target market, and how dispersed is it? In other words, is this a nationwide market or a zip code market?
- How long is a typical sales cycle? One week? One year?
- What's the average price tab? $10 or $1 million?

These types of questions drive the type of promotion you will need and the dollar amount required to penetrate and motivate your target market. The bigger the ticket, the longer the sales cycle, and the more complex the offering, the more expensive and complex the marketing campaigns will need to be.

As you grow and expand, you're likely to consider different types of creative strategies to get your customers to buy your products. Advertising and promotions strategy is a core part of your marketing plan. This section should include the general strategy as well as the detailed action items used, for example, if your strategy is to use trade publications to advertise and promote. For each targeted publication, the specifics may include the following:

- Core message for the publication
- Timetable for each advertisement or editorial—issue release date as well as deadline for the ad or editorial submission
- Copy for advertisement and creative elements
- Evaluation for publication—what are the expectations for the publication, and how will you determine if it is successful in reaching your target buyer or influencer? For example, you may measure the hits to your Web site or phone calls for information.

Using Professional Resources

There are as many types of marketing service firms as there are mediums to use. There are strategic marketing consultants, independent graphic design and writing freelancers, integrated marketing firms, advertising agencies, public relations (PR) agencies, direct-marketing firms, telemarketing firms, event planners, and specialty advertising/promotion firms. It can get quite overwhelming when you are trying to figure out how best to take your offering to market.

Let's discuss the roles as well as pros and cons of each type of organization.

- *Strategic marketing consultants.* These resources can take the form of independent contractors, boutique firms, or large, top-tier firms like the McKinsey or Boston Consulting groups. Their role is to help the executive management team determine the best course of action to obtain optimum growth potential. They may be engaged to validate a strategy, determine mergers and acquisitions (M&A) prospects, build pricing models, determine product viability, or create the 1- and 5-year strategic plans, either for fund-raising or for organic growth. You can usually work with these types of firms on either a project basis or a retainer.
- *Independent contractors or boutique firms.* These companies usually charge on a day-rate basis of anywhere between $1,200 and $3,000. Large firms can often have a minimum-size engagement of around $50,000 to $100,000 per month.
- *Freelancers.* On the other side of the spectrum are freelance graphic designers and writers. These people are a wonderful resource if you have already established your strategic plan and developed your value proposition. They are looking for very specific instructions as to what you want, so the more vague you are, the more likely you will be to have several rounds before you are satisfied. These people tend to work out of their homes and can be extremely creative but not necessarily fabulous business thinkers. Their rates will be somewhere between $45 and $150 per hour.

- *Integrated marketing firms.* These firms have a holistic approach to marketing. They have built in-house teams, strategic alliances, or both with people who have experience delivering all aspects of the marketing mix. They tend to look at the market challenge through a more collaborative, cohesive lens, understanding the functions and timing of each medium. These firms tend to be smaller in size with a more boutique feel. You may find they have certain areas of expertise such as B2B (business to business) versus B2C (business to consumer) or are industry-specific with a focus on technology, law firms, health care, and so on. You can usually work with these types of firms on either a project basis or a retainer.
- *Specialty firms (advertising, PR, direct marketing, etc.).* These firms contain experts in their fields. They have built a business doing their "thing" very well and can apply a wealth of experience in their particular medium to your business challenge. They can charge based on a project or retainer basis. (More on advertising and PR firms coming up in the chapter.)

For companies whose products are best sold via direct marketing, finding this type of expertise is also important. True direct-marketing firms know all the postal rules, have fulfillment warehouses established, and use sophisticated software systems to personalize and distribute the information, whether in a letter form or in a three-dimensional kit. They should also own or have resources for list procurement, one of the most fundamental aspects to a successful direct marketing campaign.

The pro of using any of these types of specialty firms should be obvious. If you pick the right one, they should produce fabulous results. The con is that it will take more money and more management to oversee a disperse group of providers. It can be done quite effectively, but you will probably need to assign a full-time marketing executive to manage these resources and to make sure they are all on the same message and brand strategy.

Project Basis Versus Retainer

Unless you provide services on these models, it is often confusing and intimidating to discuss the best type of payment program with a potential marketing partner. Here's how a project basis works within the firm: all work is tracked on a time basis, usually captured in 15-minute increments, like law and accounting firms use. Projects are estimated based on the detailed specs established, and time is factored by individuals required to complete the task. If the specs change, expect the price to change as well. The pros to this type of arrangement are that you only pay for the work you have authorized and that the work has a beginning and an end. The con is that the firm does not function as a strategic partner but only as a vendor, as they are not compensated to play any other role.

Retainers, on the other hand, are fixed monthly fees spread across a 12-month period. These fees are mutually established and should be assigned to specific tasks and individuals. The pros of this type of arrangement are that it gives you total flexibility to change priorities and allows the firm's leaders to fully engage in helping market your company. The con is that if you are not working with an ethical firm, time can be padded and wasted, putting more pressure on you to manage the details.

Advertising Firms

Knowing when to hire an outside ad firm can be a tricky decision. The right time could depend on your marketing and sales experience as well as your overall entrepreneurial experience launching new companies, products, and services.

In the early days, it's highly unlikely that you will need a large ad budget, let alone an ad firm. Your advertising and promotions need to be targeted and results driven. Given that most start-ups and early-stage companies have modest budgets, you may get better results by hiring a part-time advertising consultant to come in house and develop and implement initiatives. Most ad firms use a retainer-based business model and assume advertising budgets that far exceed those of most young companies. You'll end up spending more money to train a junior person in the ad firm and are likely to find that many of the best ad strategies come from your own employees, who are closer to both the products and the customers.

As you grow, you'll need to consider advertising and promotions a core part of your strategy. Most companies start with limited print or radio advertising or with direct promotions such as coupons, discounts, and other incentives, as these advertising strategies tend to be the most cost effective. You should plan to use an advertising consultant or a smaller ad firm to develop and implement this phase of your strategy. Your network and colleagues can help you find credible professionals. Additionally, take a look to see which agencies are creating campaigns that you feel are effective. Just keep in mind that any advertising and promotions strategy will need to be constantly reassessed and revised to meet changes in your marketing and overall business strategy.

Hiring an advertising firm makes sense when you are ready to conduct a major launch, whether on a local or a national basis. These firms' expertise is coming up with campaign "concepts" that best articulate your value proposition while motivating your audience to take some sort of action. You should have multiple concepts to choose from, each a distinct representation of your brand strategy. Traditional ad agencies get compensated in two ways: creative concepting and production and media planning and buying. Depending on the size of an ad budget, some firms will bundle the creative campaign work into the 15% commission fee they get for placing the spots. For this, we're probably talking media buys in the millions of dollars. The smaller the firm and the buy, the more likely you are to work on a project basis.

Public Relations

Public relations efforts can be a very cost-effective way to communicate with your target market. While it's often lumped in with advertising, it's a separate strategy and requires dedicated effort to be effective. In essence, PR is when you can get media attention for your product, service, or company through nonpaid opportunities. There are many publicists in the market, some with firms and others who operate independently.

If you believe you would be best served conducting an aggressive PR campaign, then hiring a specialist in this area makes great sense. He or she should have a Rolodex full of media contacts that cover your industry. A great PR person has built his or her reputation over years of cultivating relationships. This greatly enhances their value and effectiveness and should be appropriately compensated. If you can afford it, be sure to request senior-level talent on your account. Some firms will delegate media "pitching" to junior staff, which can damage your company's image. PR firms almost always only work on retainers, as they are providing a pure service that cannot be taken back or held up if a client doesn't pay its invoice. Therefore, these firms will usually expect to be paid upfront for the services they are providing.

PR is a great way for a young company with a unique new product to make the news on television, radio, or in print. This is, in essence, free advertising, although you may not always be able to control the message. Large companies routinely focus on promoting their image by supporting worthy charities and other causes. This in turn reinforces their brand and indirectly encourages customers to buy the company's products and services.

Finding a Good Firm

Whether you are looking for a strategic marketing consultant, an ad agency, a PR agency or a direct-mail house, the best way to find a resource is to ask others who they recommend. Talk to other business owners, call the chamber of commerce, research companies you admire and call them, use search engines, and read marketing magazines.

Before you call any of them, determine your business objective, and establish your budget. If you want to learn how to work with different types of firms, ask to meet with a principal, and tell her or him what you are trying to accomplish.

Once you've established the direction you want to go, get a list of no more than eight firms to send a request for proposal (RFP). Provide them with a high-level background on your company and your business goals. Come up with a list of questions that are important to you.

For example, you might want to know the following:

- The firm's background
- Types of clients and examples of work and results
- Bios of account members
- In-house or alliance relationships
- Average size of engagement

Review the responses and look for sloppy work, typos, and unanswered questions. Toss those immediately. Narrow your list to four contenders, and ask them to give a formal presentation. Set up 2 days of presentations in which you'll have two presentations per day: one in the morning and one in the afternoon. Make sure the executives and decision makers are all available. Ask them to give a capabilities presentation and to provide some initial thoughts on how they may approach your engagement.

Do not ask for or be swayed by "spec" creative work. If you are seeing ad concepts before there's been any kind of strategic dialogue or knowledge transfer, you are getting pretty pictures, not business-building and thoughtful marketing.

After you have seen your four presentations, narrow the field to two and go visit their offices. Ask to meet the team that will be assigned to your account. Take a tour. Does it look like a creative, organized environment or a sloppy, disheveled heap of stuff? Do the people have the appropriate appearance and "bright eyes?"

Call references and determine how they plan to kick off the relationship. Be prepared to tell the firms your budget early in the process. Don't do the "you tell me" routine. Any firm worth its reputation will give you everything it can for the dollars you have to spend. If they know what you have available, you won't get ideas you can't afford. If they don't think you've budgeted enough to accomplish your business goals, you should be told and a win-win solution established.

Guerilla Marketing

Guerilla marketing is a popular concept often associated with low-budget, early-stage companies. It can be quite successful depending on your product or service. There isn't one clear set of guerilla strategies. Rather, the term "guerilla marketing" refers to any low-cost approach. PR, for example, can be an effective guerilla marketing strategy if you manage to get noted in a magazine or on the news.

Companies are increasingly using the Internet to market their products and services. For example, we sell our products through resellers. On a regular basis (weekly, monthly, or quarterly, depending on the reseller), we create an e-mail that has some interesting information (for value) as well as limited product information. It's usually in an engaging format with graphics and links to more resources on our site. We customize our e-mail for each reseller by adding their logo and contact information. In essence, we have created a marketing tool that is turnkey. We send it to our primary marketing contact at each reseller, who in turn sends it to their entire e-mail customer distribution.

Just remember that guerilla marketing is a catchall phrase that encourages entrepreneurs and their teams to get creative on a cost-effective basis.

Developing a Sales Strategy

One of the first things you'll need to focus on in your planning is determining what kind of sales organization you'll need to develop. Different products and services require different selling solutions.

Identifying your optimal distribution strategy will help determine the type of sales organization you use. How and where do customers find and purchase your products and services? Your sales strategy will need to be suited for your distribution strategy. In my first company, we sold directly to corporations. As a result, our efforts were limited by the number of calls and meetings we could complete on a daily basis. My second and third companies operated in multiple industries. We determined that the optimal selling strategy was to align with partners and distributors in each market. Our products were complementary and provided a new revenue source for our partners, who didn't incur any product development costs. The advantage to this strategy is that you have many more sales people "selling your products," but you don't incur the cost of building a sales organization. The challenge is that your partners are likely to be selling multiple products: theirs, yours, and others. As a result, selling your products may not always be their priority. One option is to partner with your resellers and distributors to incentivize their sales team with contests, bonuses, and promotions.

Every sale strategy has its pros and cons, and you'll need to analyze them thoroughly before deciding on one. Competitor structures and strategies can also provide insight on what's likely to be successful for a specific industry.

As you develop your sales strategy, you'll need to focus on the following key areas:

- Building the optimal sales organization
- Developing sales forecasts and pipelines
- Managing your customers and your customer diversification

Building the Optimal Sales Organization

Building a sales organization takes time, and your strategy will need to account for the evolving structure. In the beginning, you're likely to have a key role in sales, and most successful entrepreneurs maintain an active involvement in the sales process even when they hire a senior team. This is one of the best ways to monitor issues and trends within your market and with your clients and sales team.

Hiring Salespeople

Most entrepreneurs will candidly tell you that it is difficult to hire good salespeople. Lots of people will tell you they are great salespeople, and most will be quite convincing as they should be. But the key issue is whether or not they can sell your product or service. Do they understand your buyer? Do they know potential buyers and have an industry network? This is particularly useful for corporate sales. Do they have experience with similar sales and cycles? Someone who sells office products is probably not going to be able to transition easily to selling complex software on a corporate-wide solution. The size of the sale, the length of the cycle, and ability to deal with the level of decision makers are all different.

One strategy that's used by many companies is hiring salespeople from their likely competitors. These candidates understand the industry, know the buyers and influencers, and are likely to produce results more quickly. Having said that, they are also likely to be more expensive and may have signed noncompete contracts with former employers. In any interview process, be sure to ask if the candidate has signed a noncompete with his or her current or former employers. If so, ask for a copy so you can properly determine the person's ability to be effective in your organization.

Monitor your sales team's results daily. There's no substitute for knowing what's going on with your market and customers. Daily monitoring helps you evaluate your team's performance better and also track changes in customer preferences. Use daily call sheets that note how many calls a salesperson made and to whom and the status of the call. Be prepared to spot-check names and numbers as there are unscrupulous salespeople who list friends or fake contacts in order to fill their sheet. Review phone bills as well to make sure calls are really being made.

When you sell to corporations and institutions, you'll need to understand how decisions are made and the budget cycles. In many cases, when you're selling to large companies, your user is often different than the final person who says yea or nay. However, you may have to first market to the user and get acceptance and the sale before selling the "value" all over again to a purchasing department. Again, the size of the sale will dictate the height of the hurdles.

Tales From the Trenches: Building a Direct Sales Force

Liz Elting, president and founder of TransPerfect, built a sales organization from scratch. She and her partner, the company's first salespeople, determined early on that they needed to have their own in-house sales team to be most successful. Rather than hiring seasoned and expensive salespeople, she opted to hire young graduates who showed promise. By investing in sales training and coaching over the course of the hire's first year, she was able to groom a successful sales team. The sales training enabled the company to make sure that each new salesperson understood the company's products, capabilities, and unique entrepreneurial culture, as well as position in the marketplace.

Early on, the company's low starting salaries resulted in turnover, which was a challenge, although a manageable one. In this case, Liz saw the benefits of the lower cost and the ability to train new candidates directly as outweighing the turnover challenge. Additionally, over time, Liz realized that much of the turnover came from young hires who came to TransPerfect directly out of college with no other corporate work experience. As a result, the company now seeks to balance its new hires to ensure that more have previous work experience. Further, as the company grew and earned an industry reputation as the largest privately held language services company in the world, it has become easier to hire more qualified and experienced candidates.

In the early days, all new sales hires received a draw against their commission for a year or more as appropriate for their sales territory. This draw was intentionally low and has remained around $25,000 to $40,000 based on the new hire's experience. The commissions are paid at 9% of the sale. As a result, the intent is to motivate the salesperson to quickly exceed their draw. Of course, there's frequent oversight to see if goals are being met and to assess any shortfalls. If a salesperson is unable to exceed his or her draw over time, then it's likely they are not a good fit with the firm. However, if someone is doing all the right things, the company will continue to work with him or her with a continued focus on results. In addition to high commissions, salespeople are incentivized by bonuses vacations, and other perks. For example, in the early days when she had only 26 employees and a banner year, Liz took the entire team to the Bahamas as a reward for the year's growth and profitability.

Managers are also incentivized with a bonus based on the revenues and profitability of his or her team. Additionally, as a market differentiator, even project and quality managers on the production side receive bonuses based on similar models. This strategy helps align everyone in delivering the best-quality services to the customer in the most cost-effective manner.

In training and motivating the sales team, Liz's company has preferred to promote from within, a strategy that has worked well. The company works hard to develop its team and twice a year holds training sessions, one in the company's New York offices and one at an off-site location. The overall sales strategy has clearly worked, as TransPerfect reached more than $200 million in sales in its 19th year of operations and has more than 57 offices around the world.

Developing Sales Forecasts and Customer Pipeline

There are essentially two ways to develop sales projections for a new venture. The first is to use industry comparables, and the second is to estimate based on market size and share.

Industry comparables are most useful if you can successfully adjust for critical variables including the age and size of the firm, size of the sales team, and marketing budget. For example, a company that projects that it can sell the same number of units in its first year of operations as its competitor, which has more than two decades in the market place, is likely to fall short.

The market share approach is similar and focuses on achieving gradual market share over 3 to 5 years. For example, if the total market for the product is $1 billion and you target achieving a market share of 1% in 3 to 5 years, then your projections would gradually build to those levels.

The challenge with these forecasting approaches is that while the revenue projections may seem doable, most entrepreneurs underestimate the cost it requires to achieve those sales. If you have 2 salespeople and your closest competitor has 10 salespeople, as well as a healthy marketing budget, you can easily begin to see why achieving the same results would be very difficult, if not impossible.

In developing your forecasts and sales strategy, it's very helpful to determine the sales revenue per employee or per salesperson. It should be consistent with the industry and your goal should be to increase it. As a general rule, if your firm tends to have higher-paid employees, it should have higher revenue per employee number. Achieving $100,000 to $200,000 in revenues per employee is common. Well-run and very profitable companies may have even more than $500,000 in revenues per employee. This number is important to monitor because it will help you realize when you have too many people on staff, with diminishing returns to revenues and possibly the bottom line. If the number decreases and revenues increase, then your team may not be as productive as you think, and you need to look at everyone's functions more closely. Your goal is for both revenues and the number to increase, although the latter may be more incremental in growth rate.

Managing Your Customers and Diversification

Plan early on how you will diversify your customer base, whether by adjusting the ratio of large and small customers or by reaching out to new industries. Be careful to ensure that one company or industry's problems won't adversely affect your firm. This customer diversification should be a core part of your early sales and marketing strategy.

Do a periodic credit check on all major customers, vendors, or suppliers. This will help you adjust your policies—particularly your payment policies—if their ratings are poor or change over time. If your business relies on several large customers, or if you sell through a few large distributors or retailers, keep abreast of how their businesses are performing and talk to their employees if you can. Their financial health will directly impact yours.

Many young companies are so happy to have customers that they don't bother to see how much each customer is costing them. Managing your customers requires customer service and marketing. Some customers can become so time consuming that you may be spending a disproportionate amount of resources servicing just one or two. Monitor how much time and money it takes to maintain a customer relationship. If you're spending 70% of your time tending to the business demands and needs of a customer who accounts for only 5% of revenues, you get the picture—something is wrong. You don't necessarily need to get rid of the customer, although some companies choose to do so, but rather you may discreetly shift resources and diplomatically realign the customer's expectations of what level of customer attention is acceptable for both.

Effective marketing and sales strategies evolve throughout the growth of your company. Paying close and frequent attention to these evolving strategies will help to ensure your long-term success.

CHAPTER 2

Managing, Governance, and Advisory

There's no shortage of books, people, and advisors who will tell you that good people are one of a company's most important assets. In working with employees, board members or advisors, make an effort to manage them well and channel their passion and talents in the same direction as yours.

Managing People

Hiring employees is one of the biggest challenges for many young companies. Issues arise from deciding which types of people you may need to hire to managing expectations as you grow. The following are some key issues to think about along the way.

Hiring: From One to Many, Many More

As you expand and begin to hire employees, take extra care before bringing on new people. Some growing companies can be in such need for people that they will hire too quickly, without a thorough hiring process in place. Having guidelines from the beginning will help avoid wrong hires. Many seasoned entrepreneurs have candidates meet with all the senior management and many of the team members that they will work with.

Your review process should include the following:

- *Résumé check.* You may want to spot check facts on the candidate's résumé to ensure accuracy. Before you start checking, get the candidate's written permission to check on her or his résumé, background, and references. You may need to fax this statement of permission before some organizations will release verification of employment or school attendance. Most companies will only formally verify or not verify employment dates. Some may release salary information, but most will not. To get more detailed information, your best bet is to talk to references—see *Reference check.* Also, check the résumé timetable for gaps. Most people have good personal reasons for gaps on their résumés, but be sure to ask. You can often tell a lot about a person by the way he or she answers. For example, some may be defensive about a time gap, while others may happily tell you they took time off to travel and find themselves. I am often happier if someone has already done their intense soul-searching—he or she is less likely to need to do it while in my company's employment.
- *Multiple interviews.* Have a prospective candidate meet with several other team members. Additionally, meet with the candidate at least twice on separate occasions. Sometimes first impressions can change for the better or worse.
- *Skills check.* If you are hiring for a specific skill, you may want to test the person. Give him or her a brief marketing or technical project to complete before the next interview. Ask him or her to consider a hypothetical problem during the interview to evaluate the candidate's thinking process and/ or ability to think on his or her feet. You can also ask to see samples of previous work or writing samples if communications are a key part of the job. Be sure that the candidate has the skill set you need and not just on the paper résumé. For fairness and accurate evaluations, be sure to ask candidates the same or very similar questions.

- *Reference check.* Always check references. A lot of people correctly assume that references will always be good. That's true—who would give the name for a bad reference? However, if you ask questions in different ways, you can glean a lot of information by how things are said or not said. Always ask if the candidate would be eligible for rehire at the old firm and if they would hire that person again. Most people are candid in their responses. Also call references; don't send letters or e-mail. People are always more candid by phone as they perceive written responses to be more legally liable.

- *Background checks.* Depending on what the employee's function will be in your company, you may want to consider some type of background check. Note that many states have guidelines about what kinds of background checks are legally permissible. Know the rules for your state and check periodically as they can change from year to year. If someone is going to be handling money, you may want to conduct a credit or criminal check. However, many states have guidelines on how you can use the information and whether or not you can keep it in the employee files.

- *Probation or trial period.* It sounds more ominous than it is, and almost all companies have a provision for a trial employment period. For most companies it is 3 months, which is usually adequate time to know if the hire is right for your firm. Most companies actually have benefits begin after this probation period. Make sure to schedule a review at the end of the 3-month period, so that both you and the employee can be sure that the position is right for both of you. This probation or trial period policy should be stated in your employee manual, a copy of which should be provided to all hires.

Successful hires are dependent on getting not only the right skills but also the right personality fit. Consider a candidate based on her or his suitability for the company, not just a specific job. Does the candidate have the right work attitude and ethic to fit in with your firm? If people work in close quarters or need to be flexible and work on different teams, it's essential that they get along. Sometimes, it can just be a case of a personality fit. If you hire someone who quickly seems to not fit the organization, you may need to take immediate action. Use the trial employment period to meet to discuss the employee's style and the company culture. If a couple of meetings over the first month or two do not seem to be working, you may need to terminate the employee rather than let discontent grow and widen. The productivity of the rest of your team may be negatively impacted if a new hire can't and won't fit in.

With new employees, use both a new hire letter and a confidentiality or noncompete letter. The new hire letter should state the person's employment is "at will" and while employed, the new hire has a salary and other basic benefits. (See the Sample Template for Offer Letter.) Don't add too much detail or make binding promises. While this provision has been standard for all companies, many firms find that their ability to exercise their "at-will" provision is increasingly limited.

After you have a couple of employees, it's worth implementing an employee manual. A lawyer should be able to provide the basic form of one that you can customize if needed. Your employee manual should state the details of any benefits. Remember that you don't need to provide overly generous benefits and privileges. A basic manual will state working hours, dress code, if applicable, policy toward discrimination and harassment, and any procedures for addressing office issues. Manuals can and should be updated annually or once every 2 years to reflect changes in the company.

The employment at-will provision is simply to provide you flexibility in case you need to fire someone for cause or not for cause. Remember, you can't ever fire an employee for discriminatory or retaliatory reasons. If you need to terminate an employee—and almost every entrepreneur will have to at some point in his or her company's growth—conduct a professional and tactful termination meeting. Always have at least one other senior manager present, preferably from human resources (HR).

If the issues are skills-based, you should have already conducted one or more performance reviews in which you met with the employee to discuss the problem areas. Document the meeting and action items that need improvement. Once an employee fails to improve, you'll have cause and be able to terminate employment without facing legal actions.

Sample Template for Offer Letter

DATE

Dear _____:

It is with great pleasure that we extend to you the following offer:

Position:
Annual Salary:
Vacation: _____ vacation days
All federal holidays (this is optional)
Effective Date:
Start Date:

These compensation terms are conditioned upon your continued employment with XYZ Company. In accordance with XYZ Company's policy, your employment is "at will" and may be terminated, with or without cause, at any time at the option of XYZ Company or you.

You will be receiving, under separate cover, information related to health insurance and benefits and will be eligible for health insurance coverage effective_____.

Regards,

_____

Your employee manual should outline the specifics regarding what is and isn't "cause" for terminating an employee as well as standard benefits relating to days off, and so on. You should have a lawyer review or create your manual for you as it is the official set of guidelines for employees. It will also obviously contain language about not discriminating and equal opportunity. Most lawyers will tell you that less is best and that you should provide clear guidelines for both the company and the employee on the terms of employment. Spend some time giving the manual the right tone. You will probably need to modify it from time to time.

If you have proprietary products or technology, you should implement a confidentiality agreement. Many companies also opt to have salespeople sign confidentiality and noncompete agreements.

Corporate Culture

Pay particular attention early on to establishing a corporate culture that is both complementary to your management style and to the needs of your company and employees. Different industries and talents require distinct cultures in which to flourish. Don't wait until things get sour to think about culture. Nurture it from the beginning.

In building a corporate culture, there are many similarities. Culture is a set of shared values and attitudes. Corporate cultures are really the company's personality and include everything from determining the dress code and physical ambiance of the office to the ways employees interact and relate to one another and to you and other senior managers.

Think about what kind of corporate culture you want to promote. How do employees perceive you? What kind of environment do you work in best? Manage in best? The answers to these questions are likely to greatly influence the culture. If you have one or more partners, it's particularly important to have a consistent culture. If your management styles and business values are very different, it can be confusing for your employees, who may get mixed messages. Invariably one of you is likely to have a stronger influence on the corporate culture, for better or worse, and hopefully for better. Make the effort to discuss these issues early on as you add employees to the office.

Never underestimate the impact of the outside world on your workforce. It shapes their expectations of themselves as an employee and of you as the employer. In good economic times, obviously the demands increase, and in recessions, while the demands decrease, so too does overall morale. The outside world impacts productivity, customer service, and overall enthusiasm. This should not be news to you. Considering all factors that impact your workforce is basic management. Unfortunately, many entrepreneurs forget to incorporate basic management practices and thinking into their daily management style. It's always more relevant to younger companies as these issues can be become more magnified and disrupt the bottom line much more quickly in a small company than in a larger company where groups of employees are more segregated from each other.

Corporate culture is also impacted by the structure of the organization. In the early days, you're likely to be very lean, and everyone will need to multitask nimbly. As you grow and add people, specific job responsibilities will become more defined. You'll find that some employees may thrive better in one type of environment versus another, and others are able to transition. Employees who love the freshness of multitasking may become bored and lose work performance if their job becomes narrowly defined. On the other hand, some people do best when they know the specific tasks associated with their job and like to remain within well-defined parameters. You will need both types of people. Be aware of who on your growing team fits in which category and who fits in the shades between.

As part of defining and communicating your corporate culture, most companies find it useful to write down the company's values and mission. Make sure as you go through this process that your mission statement reflects principals that you (and any partners) sincerely embrace. If it's just a paper exercise, your employees will not pay it much attention. It's helpful to have these principles noted not only in public areas (like a poster in the common area or, if appropriate for public access, on the Web site) but also in the employee manual.

Access

In the beginning, you're likely to have a more junior or more technical team. You'll probably spend a great deal of time with each person, often working in close quarters as space is usually limited. These people are essential to your early growth and most will take great pride in knowing that they were the "ground crew," so to speak.

The challenge occurs when you begin to add more people to the team and have less time and attention to give to people who have come to expect it. You may also hire more senior people, creating management layers that will limit the ground crew's access to you. This will occur even if you maintain an open-door style of management. It's just simply an inevitable aspect of growing. The key is to manage the expectations of this group of people. Find ways to communicate regularly, either through e-mails or newsletters. Often people who enjoyed "being in the know" resent no longer being first in line for communication. Make it a point to recognize their work and efforts, publicly if possible. During the dot-com boom, many early-stage companies gave each hire a number based on the order of when she or he started working. This sense of historical hierarchy helped to mitigate the angst that many felt from the natural and inevitable corporate changes.

Expectations

Managing employee expectations as you grow can be both rewarding and challenging.

The weekly Friday pizza party that was just fine for 5 employees is going to start eating into your budget at 50 employees and be financially unreasonable for 100 employees. In my second company, in the beginning, we used to celebrate every person's birthday with an office cake. It worked fine while we were at an inexpensive 8-inch cake from our local grocery store, which happened to taste pretty good. Once we passed about 10 people and the cake size changed, we realized that celebrating *every* birthday was too costly. We opted to celebrate birthdays once a month, and instead of getting one big custom bakery cake, which would have become very expensive, we chose several of the 8-inch options.

Your perks will need to be adjusted as you grow and you may get some resistance on some changes. The cake example worked out fine in the end. On the other end, it's possible that people will get annoyed as some benefits are reduced or modified as the employee population grows. I know many colleagues who have experienced what I call the "hot cocoa and coffee variety challenge." It starts when, in the early days, you may offer a variety of benefits like beverages, snack foods, and tissue boxes for each desk. Companies usually do this to keep break times quick and employees focused on the work at hand. Some companies that expect late nights from their employees may also keep well stocked kitchens to keep people at their desks. Over time, you'll realize that instead of five or six varieties of coffee, two should suffice. One type of tea will do instead of stocking a full assortment. Many entrepreneurs face this type of situation and find that when they try cutting nonessential expenses, there can be employee dissatisfaction.

This is not an unusual scenario. It happens even to the largest and most established of companies who have to reduce some perks in times of cost cutting. I point it out here because most entrepreneurs are unprepared for the backlash. Entrepreneurs who provide these benefits in the early days are more used to the positive feedback and are unaware that changing times may require adjustments, even of the smaller and less significant items. Some entrepreneurs prefer to not provide these items as daily benefits but as exceptions so that no one takes them for granted.

Employee Benefits

There is a wide range of federal and state guidelines in the United States that govern benefits regarding parental leave, jury duty, military leave, and so on. You'll need to consult with a labor lawyer to identify the guidelines that apply to your size of company. Also project out at least 12 to 24 months, and make a note of the types of guidelines that may apply once you have reached certain benchmarks on the number of full-time and part-time employees.

It may help you plan your staffing needs more efficiently to hire more part-time or project workers, for whom many of the guidelines may not apply. Early-stage companies often prefer to use "temporary" or "project workers" instead of hiring them as employees. In general, most companies do not pay taxes for temporary or project workers, often called consultants. Instead companies give a gross payment, based on a negotiated hourly, weekly, or monthly rate. The Internal Revenue Service (IRS) has guidelines that define a full-time employee and that state when payroll processing and taxes are required. Your accountant can help you understand the way taxes may impact your staffing plan.

Many young companies find that they can acquire senior skill sets by hiring skilled individuals as part-timers. For example, they may hire a part-time chief financial officer (CFO) or HR manager. Many of these jobs are essential for building strong, viable organizations in the long term; however, there's rarely enough full-time work for these professionals. Many Web sites can help you find this senior level of part-time professional.

Medical, Dental, and Life

Most growing companies find it advantageous to offer some type of medical benefits, often because the entrepreneur needs these personally. You will also find that having some sort of medical coverage is an important recruitment tool. You may lose valuable potential employees who need coverage and who may even be willing to pay for it themselves. In the United States, most insurance companies will provide medical plans for young companies with at least two employees being covered.

You can decide what constitutes an eligible employee based on his or her employment start date and the number of hours the person works per week. Most companies choose to offer medical benefits to employees who work at least 30 hours per week and have been employed with the company for a minimum of 3 months, although some may wait till 6 months. Part of this decision depends on whether your company pays for a portion of the expense or if the employee pays for all of it on a pretax basis. If you are in your early years and not certain of your profitability, your best bet is to offer medical coverage but let the cost be 100% covered by the employee. It may not be a well-liked policy, but it helps to manage expectations as you grow and need flexibility with costs. As you grow and become more financially stable, you may opt to cover up to 50% of the expense, which is pretty standard. It's rare these days, but some companies do cover 100% of the expense. This is often industry-specific and further, if you have union employees, there may be additional considerations that you need to be aware of.

Some companies choose to provide additional employee benefits in the form of life insurance, disability, and travel accident insurance. In general, remember it's always easier to give more coverage as you grow and much harder to reduce benefits. Most employees are aware of the financial limitations of young companies and will be more tolerant of fewer benefits earlier on.

As you grow, you may want to consider using the services of employee benefits administrators and consulting firms to determine which benefits fit your company's budget and make you competitive from a hiring perspective. Many of these firms will manage the benefits for you for a fee.

Vacation, Sick Leave, and Holidays

In the United States, depending on the number of employees you have, you may be required to provide unpaid sick leave for medical or family leave. Most professionals coming from the corporate world are accustomed to a number of paid sick days. You'll need to determine what works best for your growing company.

Over the years, from talking with many entrepreneurs and owners of young firms, I have found that combining personal and sick days allows employees the most flexibility and does not penalize those who tend not to get sick or stay home for minor ailments. For example, we give five combined paid personal or sick days for each employee. These days do not include maternity or disability leaves. On the off chance that an employee is sick for more than 5 days, then he or she begins to use up vacation days. Some companies prefer to have illness periods instead of days. For example, three illnesses a year, whether it is 1 day or 5 days. This way, someone who has the flu for a week does not use up vacation days. All these benefits incur costs, so determine the mix that makes best sense for your company, employees, and industry.

When determining your company's vacation and sick leave, you should always retain the option and right under your employee manual to make exceptions at the company's discretion. However, if this becomes an ongoing issue modify your leave policy, as you do not want to make exceptions a habit.

Vacation days are usually based on seniority and range from 10 to 20 days per year. Most young companies find it costly and cumbersome to let vacation, personal, and sick days accrue to the next year. Accordingly, "use it or lose it" policies are standard for young companies just as they are for many established larger firms. You may want to see what is standard for each position in your industry, and award vacation and sick days accordingly.

A perk that is often very well appreciated by many employees is the opportunity to take their birthday as a holiday. Some companies offer a rotating birthday holiday so that the employee can choose to take their own birthday or that of another immediate family member. This can be a great way to build goodwill with your team.

Most companies give major holidays as paid time off to their employees. You'll need to see what works best for your company and industry. For example, if your customers expect 24/7 service, who will manage issues on holidays? Young companies often manage this by having a more general policy in place providing e-mail customer response within a set time frame, such as two business days, not including holidays. You'll still need to assign coverage, but it will be less onerous. You may also consider staggering the holidays employees can take or make it volunteer-based for the popular ones like Thanksgiving, Christmas, and New Year's.

Bonuses

Bonuses can come in many forms: cash, stock (which I'll discuss in the next section), vacation days, company and group events and outings, and so on. The first step is to determine what you want bonuses to mean to your employees. Is it recognition of outstanding achievement and therefore an award for few but not for all? Or is a bonus an annual "thank-you" to all employees for jobs well done? In countries like Japan, which focus on the collective spirit of a company, traditionally every employee gets a year-end and a midyear bonus that is based on a predetermined multiple of her or his weekly salary. In some industries, like finance and investment banking, bonuses represent a form of profit sharing, and each employee's take is based on a predetermined formula of her or his contribution to the revenues and bottom line.

You may want to take a look at your competitors to see what their policies and benefits are. At the minimum, you want to be competitive in your ability to hire the best candidates. At best, an innovative approach might help you stand apart if you compete heavily in the market for the best employees. As with other employee programs and benefits, consistency is key. You can always add more in later years, but don't be overly generous one year only to have to completely pull back from any bonuses in the next down year.

You can use a bonus as a way to motivate everyone to repeat the year's successes. Be sure that you set aside a good portion of the year's profits to grow the company rather than distribute it to employees entirely.

Cash is one of the more traditional bonus rewards. Some companies give gifts at key holidays—for example, a turkey for every employee at Thanksgiving or Christmas. Remember that every form of bonus has a cost, and you'll need to think about not only how it impacts your bottom line, but if it meets the expectations of your employees and is in line with your industry. Some may love the holiday turkey, and others would prefer a significant cash gift. Another option used by many companies is gift cards, for example from Visa, MasterCard, American Express, Amazon, or Starbucks. In some cases, these can be purchased in bulk and at a discount. Again, you'll need to understand what your employees will value.

Recent studies have shown that most employees prefer bonuses in the form of extra vacation days. This is usually one of the most economical ways for entrepreneurs to reward valued employees. While there is still a technical cost—the actual wages and benefits for the day or days the employee receives—it is not an additional new cost. The employee's wages and benefits are already part of your firm's budget. Chances are that valued and conscientious workers, for whom you'd be considering bonus time off, are also likely to be sure to complete all their work, so there are no loose ends or unmet customer needs. Many employees may just relish being awarded the extra bonus time off and may not take it for months.

Additional incentives are vacations, meals, and trip vouchers. Company events and outings are a great way to reward the team as well as to encourage employees to get to know one another and to build loyalty. Some companies have an annual holiday party in December. Some invite families and others limit it to employees. Part of your decision will be based on budget considerations and whether you can host the event at your office or if you need to rent outside space. If you are having a holiday event for clients, plan a separate one for employees.

Stock

Stock is an additional form of compensation for employees. It can be used to reward valuable employees as well as to encourage loyalty from early employees who may be making less than market salaries or have to put in significantly more work time. There are three forms of stock compensation. The most commonly known is the stock option. Lesser known but quite useful are stock appreciation rights and actual outright stock purchases. I'll discuss all three.

Many companies, particularly those that are funded by private investment from angels or venture capitalists, establish stock ownership plans. Stock ownership has become a very common incentive tool, particularly for senior hires. Stock options actually give the employee the right to buy the stock at a specified price for a certain period of time. These options can also be exercised if the company is acquired. Once purchased, this stock represents actual ownership in the company.

For many employees of public companies, this can be a lucrative form of compensation. For employees of young, nonpublic companies, the issue is the time it may take for this benefit to have actual financial value. Further, the value of options can disappear quickly and can take years to reacquire value. Unless you have a growth company with very strong potential either in the stock market or for being acquired, your employees may not all value receiving stock options.

On average, most companies reserve around 15% of the company's stock for employees. There are no hard-and-fast rules and obviously you should not give up the whole 15% early on. This number may get diluted by future rounds of fund-raising, depending on the terms of each round and your negotiating ability. Dilution means that the stocks held by any investor or employee represents a smaller percentage of the equity as new shares are given to new investors. In this case, in the early days you may reserve 15% of the shares for employees, but with your next round of funding this may go down to less than 15%.

As an employee of the company, you can choose to participate in the employee plan. Some entrepreneurs and venture capitalists (VCs) see stock options as a way to get some equity back to the entrepreneur for a job well done. Options are usually priced higher than the current value or are triggered in the event of an acquisition.

Stock appreciation rights enable employees to receive financial payment if a stock appreciates, but they don't have to actually exercise the option. Some companies choose to give stock directly, but this is less commonly used than options.

If you are the sole owner of your company, you can incent your team with similar concepts without giving up equity. Some entrepreneurs implement a form of profit sharing or financial benefit if the company is sold. This enables employees to benefit in the upside without the entrepreneur giving up equity. This is a more realistic option if you're not intending to go public or be acquired in the next 5 years. You can always add a new stock plan as you grow and initial public offerings (IPOs) or acquisitions become more realistic exit strategies. Remember, the goal is to provide incentive and reward for your employees. They should perceive value in a reasonable time horizon.

Governance and Advisory

There are two types of groups that provide governance and advice: a board of directors and an advisory board, sometimes called an advisory council or group. The operative word is "advisory." Everyone tells you to set up a board and advisory council, but many entrepreneurs don't pay enough attention to establishing truly useful boards. Board and advisory members can be enormously beneficial if they are selected, cultivated, and utilized wisely.

Board of Directors

Legally, most types of companies must have a board of directors. However, many young companies do not necessarily institute one until they receive external funding—usually venture capital. Boards of directors primarily have a fiduciary duty. With the increased threat of litigation from many angles, many potential board members may be initially reluctant to take on this role as it brings on legal obligations.

Your first set of board members is likely to be your investors, whether friends and family, angels, or venture capitalists. When you get to the venture capital or "institutional" stage of investors, you may find that your new members would prefer not to be on a board filled with friends and family and will help start the process of finding more professional board members to fill key slots. This can be quite helpful in getting people with access and experience involved with your firm. However, be aware that some of them may have allegiances to your venture capitalist, often as a result of other deals, and that some may not be able to retain objectivity in challenging scenarios. Board members can have their own agendas that may not be in your interest (as you'll read in the example at the end of this chapter).

Boards of directors should provide expertise and outreach, particularly VC board members, to customers, vendors, and key industry members. They can provide references for accessing lawyers, accountants, investors, and investment bankers.

To recruit board members, you'll need to get board liability insurance, usually called D & O insurance (directors and officers). This has become even more relevant in the past decade as seasoned professionals are well aware of the potential liabilities if they serve on a corporate board. Many professionals may prefer to serve on an advisory board that has no fiduciary responsibilities. Once they are comfortable with a company's operations, they may agree to serve on the board. In such situations be clear on what you expect from members of either type of board and whether you will need them to switch eventually.

Use the process outlined below to identify a plan for each board member to bring in sales or know how to help grow the company.

Advisory Boards

Many companies use advisory boards as a way to gain insight, expertise, and contacts. In some industries, the advisory board may be a technical advisory board providing scientific or technical expertise. While less common, some companies may have both a general advisory board and a technical advisory board. For example, a biotech firm might have two distinct needs: one on the scientific side and the other on the sales and marketing side.

Be wary of just assembling a list of names, no matter how credible. Just as there is for your board of directors, there should be a clear mission for the group and a plan for each member. Educate board members thoroughly on your firm, and establish mutual expectations. People serve on advisory boards more for the industry outreach rather than for a monetary compensation. You can give advisory members warrants or other equity incentives.

Tales From the Trenches

As chief executive officer (CEO) of a hot, growing branding firm in Atlanta, Karen See of Abovo Group successfully built an advisory board without giving up any equity. Members found value in networking with others on the board as well as with Karen, who often introduced members to others in the local business community. Advisory board members were also likely intrigued by Abovo because it was a hot growth company, and it had been named the fourth fastest growing female-owned business in Atlanta in 2000.

Deciding whom to ask to be board members required some strategic planning, however. Karen made a list of the people she wanted and put a sales plan together for getting them. It started with her former boss and mentor, Larry Ferguson, who was the former CEO of First Data Corporation, Health Systems Division. Even though Larry lived in Charlotte, he was willing to travel to Atlanta once a quarter to help because he had been the one to encourage her to start the business in 1997 and had been her first client. In Atlanta, Karen focused on getting Tom McNeight, CEO of GuardedNet. Tom was one of the city's top technology executives, and people were always trying to find a way to be introduced to him. Karen used Larry to get Tom, and Tom was used to get the remaining board members. Once these people knew who else was on board, they quickly agreed.

Karen made an effort to make meetings engaging, strategic, and focused. She'd fax or e-mail agendas and detailed strategic information a few days in advance. She openly solicited and encouraged members to offer innovative suggestions for all parts of her fast growing company. Having grown to almost 100 employees in just 3 years, she wanted input on management issues as well as overall strategy. She shared everything with her board, from the financials to HR issues to sales opportunities to strategic growth plans. But she never forgot that these board members were also a sales channel, so dwelling on the negative was not good for getting new business.

Her board gave her candid feedback on her strategic plans as well as helped interview new executive applicants. As CEOs often find, getting useful and positive feedback can be rare. Her board provided the positive reinforcement and encouragement executives need. They not only helped her manage the growth, but they helped her successfully manage her way through the economic downturn that hurt so many marketing firms—particularly those with a heavy technology client base.

Compensating a board of advisors of this caliber can be daunting. Karen realized that most of the members were financially well-off, so she decided to compensate them with creative rather than financial incentives. She gave quarterly gift cards for things like fine dining and a year-long subscription to a business book-of-the-month club as a way to say thank you.

While the roles of boards of directors and advisory boards differ in some areas, many factors are actually quite similar. Issues relating to recruitment, plan development, education, compensation, and evaluation overlap. I'll cover these below and highlight any differences. Boards are only useful if you plan and utilize them strategically.

Recruiting

The optimal candidates for boards depend in large part on your industry and the stage of your company. Focus on an advisory board first, as it will eliminate the need to address the candidate's fiduciary responsibilities and, accordingly, the compensation component may be less.

An industry expert brings credibility to young companies. You may also want to consider people with industry sales, marketing, and distribution expertise. Many companies also seek out professionals in law, finance, and accounting to provide valuable expertise at critical junctures. You may also want to add one or more entrepreneurs. Look for people with not only industry expertise but experience in successful and unsuccessful ventures. We live in a culture where successes are valued more, but it's the failures that can provide essential lessons. Don't underestimate this group of people, especially if they have other complementary skills in addition to raising capital and industry experience.

To attract credible candidates, you'll need to have a formal business plan and perhaps even a PowerPoint presentation. Advisory board member candidates may even be suitable angel investors, but be clear in defining both of their roles to avoid confusion and frustrations. If they do invest, be clear that the advisory board role is for a finite time period and the investment did not buy them a lifetime seat. This is where a clear manual can be very helpful. Term limits are a useful management tool. As one of my lawyers once reminded me—you can always make exceptions to a term limit, but it's at your discretion and is not their automatic expectation.

As you build your boards, you will often find it easier to attract new people. Seasoned professionals often see boards as a way to meet and network with other industry experts. If you have some strong members, use this as a recruiting tool.

Set a Plan

As you begin to develop your board, outline your strengths and weaknesses. You need board members who can help fill in gaps in terms of networks, experience, and expertise. The plan should highlight the kinds of board members who could provide value and at what stages of the company's growth. This will help you time your recruiting efforts for the right stage of the company. Board and advisory members need to feel useful, and bringing them on too soon could frustrate both of you and limit their involvement when you need it most.

When you begin to recruit potential members, outline a plan for each candidate. Be specific and realistic in the action items. Start by stating modest expectations for what you want the member to do. For example, you may need introductions to one or more specific key customers. You may also want a monthly coffee hour with that person for general advice and strategy planning. This can be more useful if your company is still young and you need senior guidance in several areas, for example, internal management, financial, and sales and marketing. Specific action items and goals will actually help your board member feel useful and begin to provide value quickly.

Include expectations such as attending meetings in your plan. Indicate whether board members will receive compensation or expense reimbursement. Also, you may want to clearly state the term for serving on either type of board. Clarity will help you avoid any misunderstandings.

Educate

As you approach and recruit board members, you're likely to focus on people who know your industry, but remember that they probably don't know much about your company.

You may find it helpful to prepare a binder of information that includes the following:

- Summary of the company's mission and executive summary
- Business plan (including financial projections as well as recent historical financial statements)
- Marketing and sales plan (include key target customers)
- General board plan and guidelines (include information on board meetings and terms for members)
- List of other board members with contact information and a brief background paragraph on each
- Brief, one-page plan for the specific board member
- Information on options, if applicable
- Samples of marketing materials and products

Some companies also provide each board member with a business card. It's a great way to expand your company's reach and enable board members to more easily network on the company's behalf.

As your overall strategy and plan evolve, be sure to communicate it to board members. They can only be useful if they are up-to-date on strategy, new clients, products, and corporate successes.

Compensation

Initially, board and advisory members are compensated with small amounts of equity, usually in the form of warrants. If and when you establish an employee stock option, you'll want to have some guidelines for this group of people as well. Be careful not to give away too much equity in the early days. You need to pace yourself and make sure everyone is impacted evenly. Any dilution from raising more equity should occur later on.

Additionally, you'll probably want to consider some compensation or reimbursement for attending meetings. Karen See of the Abovo Group used gift cards from popular retail establishments like Starbucks and Borders. Her advisory board consisted of very successful professionals, and as a result, they were motivated not by financial compensation but rather by the thrill of helping to guide a very fast growing and publicly visible company. The gifts usually were in the $100 range and were meant to be more of a token of appreciation for the time and expertise the board was providing.

Evaluation

As part of your board plan, you should consider how you'll evaluate the role of each member to ensure that it's mutually beneficial. I've heard countless stories of board members who, rather than contributing to the company, ended up asking favors of the entrepreneur and the company's employees. Whether the board member asks for introductions, a job, or help creating a Web site, you'll have to determine if they are continuing to provide value or are becoming a drain and distraction.

As you build your boards, you'll need to pay close and discreet attention to each member's personal motivations and how these may evolve over time.

Overall, there are many good and bad stories of boards' impact on entrepreneurs. Most entrepreneurs are reluctant to publicly disclose the details of this private business forum, but if you can have someone to privately tell you about her or his board, the stories can be illuminating. It's important to know your board members well—not just their professional experience but also how effective they have been on other boards and in previous executive roles as well as their personal ambitions.

One team of entrepreneurs learned the importance of such fact finding the hard way when one of their trusted board members of 5 years used his knowledge of the company and customers to their detriment. When the company came upon challenging economic times, he quietly used his relationships with other board members to tip the company into Chapter 7 bankruptcy and purchase the assets for a deep discount. He reestablished the company under a new name and his ownership and installed himself as the CEO. He could have just demanded a restructuring before investing more money, but his personal motivations inspired him to use a different tactic. Sound farfetched? Perhaps, but it is also a true and bitter experience for many entrepreneurs, although not always with the board member themselves as the new corporate head; it can also be another board member, an outside professional, or sometimes a family member.

Venture capitalists have been known to carry out maneuvers like this one without the semblance of any personal motivation. Usually VCs will do this if the company is in trouble and the VC is unwilling to put in new money without this type of restructuring. The entrepreneur is often aware of the process, even if he or she is not part of the new company.

Board members and employees are all valuable assets that need to be well managed. Make an effort from the early days to draft a plan for how you will grow both your employee base and your boards of directors and advisors.

CHAPTER 3

Entrepreneurship on the Fly

As your company becomes established and grows, you will have to establish processes, procedures, and plans, all of which will need to be modified many times due to external as well as internal changes. How you manage and what kinds of processes and structures you implement will depend in large part on your firm, its stage of growth, your industry, and the state of the economy. In this chapter, I'll highlight the kinds of issues you should be aware of as you navigate bumps in the road and experience different stages of growth. Even with the best of planning, you'll need to be able to think fast—effectively and efficiently—and respond to challenges and opportunities with creativity, flexibility, and speed. It's what I call "entrepreneurship on the fly."

Navigating the Bumps in the Road

The key for most entrepreneurs is to know that they are not alone. Most entrepreneurs worry at least once in their journey that no one else has made the mistakes or faced the challenges that they face. The reality is that no matter what kind of mistake you made or what kind of scenario you're facing, you're probably in good company. Lots of businesses have their ups and downs, and lots of businesses go through growth cycles. Good entrepreneurship is all about navigating the bumps and restructuring or redirecting.

As you grow, continuously assess your policies, products, procedures, and even people. Be willing to let go of whatever is no longer working or effective. It's often most difficult to get rid of people and products. We get attached to both—usually because they have a face and personality and spirit. And yes, I am talking not just about the people but the products too.

Understand that you *will* encounter several cycles—business cycles, sales cycles, economic cycles, and product cycles—and be ready for them as best you can.

Business and Sales Cycles

Every business experiences cycles. No business is ever in an up cycle all the time. In fact, the longer you've been around, the more likely you are to experience higher peaks and lower valleys. While you can't always avoid a market downturn, you can monitor your market well enough to anticipate challenges before they become crises.

Toward this end, you should find a key number in your business that tells you if your sales are on track or off. Some people monitor shipments, while others monitor days of inventory. In my business, we monitor the inventory of our resellers. We initially tracked the dollar volume of sales but found that the number of units in their inventory was far more telling. For example, one reseller booked revenues because products were sold, but the products were not actually distributed to the customer. As a result, we experienced sales slowdowns because they didn't need to reorder the product quickly enough. By focusing on units instead of revenues booked, we could pinpoint distribution problems as well as anticipate sales slowdowns and work with our resellers and partners accordingly.

Also, if you do use resellers, pay close attention to their profitability and how their salespeople are incentivized to sell your products versus others that they carry. If the salespeople make more money from selling other products, guess which ones they will push harder—even if the products are not competitive. Pay close attention to your reseller or distributor's sales structure and process.

Make the effort to focus on existing customers. They're likely to generate your most cost-effective new sales. It's common to hear that it costs five times as much to get a new customer than to keep an existing one and grow them. Focus on your most profitable customers with the best margins. At the same time, there's a delicate balancing act of focusing on both managing your current customers while filling your sales pipeline and diversifying your customer base.

Focusing on diversifying your customer base from day one is essential. A downturn in sales to one major client often tips young companies into failure. Even the government can't remain a reliable majority customer. Strive to have no single customer account for more than 10% of your total revenues. This will help minimize your pain when your clients stumble. Many career entrepreneurs take the idea of diversification one step further and get involved with or fund another company once their first company is growing and stable.

As you grow, treat all of your customers and potential customers with kindness and respect. Sometimes fast-growing companies turn away business for varying reasons. For example, the customer is too small or is not profitable enough. When you experience your bumps in the road, you may want to take on some of these customers. Make sure they still want to do business with you.

Product Cycles: Diversify and Innovate

This may sound basic, but many companies enjoying the success of their new product or service forget to think about what's next. You need new products or new versions of your products to keep customers interested in your company. The frequency with which you develop new products or services depends on your customer and industry. But whether you innovate every year or once every 5 years, always remember to plan for the next success.

It's also important to differentiate between product and corporate loyalty. One of the secrets of truly successful and enduring companies is the ability to not get attached to their "products or service." Your business should be based on satisfying a customer need. When your customers need a change in your product or service, you'll be able to act proactively rather than reactively. Your passion should be directed toward building a long-lasting company focused on meeting customers' needs, not a long-lasting product.

Managing

If you worked for a company before you started your own venture, think back to how you viewed corporate life and management when you weren't in a management position. Fast-forward to the days that you were a manager or executive and think of how you viewed business processes. Then speed ahead to the present, where you're now an owner. Business can look very different from all three perspectives, and it's important to keep this in mind. When you're an employee, it's easy to blame "management" for everything. When you're a manager, the board, chief executive officer (CEO), owners, and even employees can seem like good targets. When you're an owner, well, you get the picture; it's the others who lack the loyalty and commitment and who demand too much from a young, growing company.

The biggest difference in perspectives comes down to loyalty and ownership. Entrepreneurs tend to think of their companies as their "children" and to think that those "children" need undivided attention and nurturing. Career entrepreneurs may be slightly more experienced in keeping a Chinese wall between their ventures and their personal emotions and world, but even then their companies are still their passion. For many employees, let's face it, it's just a job. Even if they love their jobs, as many do, it's still just a job, and they can leave and will do so if they need to. Even investors are likely to regard your business as just one of a number of deals. Balancing these varying perspectives between the different stakeholders is critical. Strive to see issues from all perspectives so that you keep a balanced approach to management and are more likely to make the fairest and best decision for all.

Employee Issues

Most entrepreneurs will tell you that as they ramp up and progress, the people issues increasingly dominate their time. Every company has a workforce diverse not only in race and gender but also in terms of skills, commitment, loyalty, and personality. Finding, keeping, and motivating the best people are perhaps the hardest tasks for entrepreneurs. Keeping different perspectives in mind, think about the kind of company you would like to work in and then attempt to create the culture, the processes, and the compensation systems that reflect that kind of work environment. Young companies operate best when their culture is based on a meritocracy: a culture that prizes capabilities and results. Integrity drives most people to do the best that they can. Understand the difference between intent and outcome.

As you start to grow, you'll need to pay close attention to how employees manage the growth process. Some get used to the perks of being part of a small company—for example, having close proximity and easy access to you, the founder and president. Managing employee expectations is critical, and it's a daily process. People, especially the ground crew, will expect the same perks, treatment, and access as you grow. It's not likely that you can maintain the same level of perks, and it may not even be desirable to do so. Pay attention to the human resources (HR) component. Have weekly meetings with your employees to help them understand what is going on or what to expect. If meetings aren't doable or efficient, sending e-mail updates at regular intervals helps. Sometimes you need to go out of your way to provide some personal attention to valued employees to help them along the way. I should note that providing personal attention does not mean becoming close friends with employees. If you become friends with your employees, it may be very hard to address tough business issues like poor performance. You may even need to fire them at some point. Keep a professional distance, at least for a few years, until you're sure that performance will not be an issue.

With senior hires, it's important to recognize that growth companies tend to have strong entrepreneurial cultures and are usually led by strong entrepreneurs. It can be hard for senior outside managers to fit into companies with strong entrepreneurs and distinct operating cultures. Additionally, they may not always understand how best to manage others in this type of environment. Outline clear roles and responsibilities and monitor them often in the first year to ensure there's a good fit.

Focus on helping your employees understand the culture of a young, growing, entrepreneurial company. Review customers, revenues, and expenses with the entire team. Start early on, and teach your team to watch expenses so that, as you grow, everyone is paying attention to cost control and doesn't become complacent. Often, there are more wasted expenses when companies grow quickly, as everyone tends to be more focused on revenues than on expenses. Help your employees understand how businesses become sustainable and the relationship among revenues, expenses, and profits. You may find that your employees even generate ideas over time to increase profits as well keep costs down.

Sometimes people are reluctant to be innovative not because they don't have good ideas, but because they're afraid of failure or of offering dumb ideas. Encourage your team to make suggestions, no matter how wild. You may want to consider incentives for new ideas. These incentives may include small bonuses of a couple hundred dollars. Often what employees really want is public recognition for their contributions. You may have an employee of the week or month award or a "Great Idea" certificate the employee can display when he or she has contributed to the company. Ideas that get implemented may warrant additional congratulatory attention depending on the corporate impact. Small but meaningful gestures go a long way toward making everyone feel as if he or she is a critical member of the entrepreneurial team.

Institutionalize Decisions and Processes

Expect to experience turnover. Have people learn multiple functions wherever possible. Also work to institutionalize decisions and processes as much as possible. Many young companies fail to do this in the early days and then when a key employee leaves, there's often a gap in institutional knowledge.

Keep detailed files on how a decision is made and what analysis and process was used to create things like pricing, marketing campaigns, and product designs. If your new hires are going to be effective, they need to know the company's history so they can challenge assumptions and decisions as appropriate.

The reality is that everyone can be replaced. Even presidents come and go. As a result, your focus should be on institutionalizing a function or job and not making it fit a particular person. Even in the best of circumstances, employees may leave your company, often for personal reasons, not just financial. If you have crafted job descriptions and spent some time putting policies and procedures in place, then replacing even talented people should be more straightforward. When you're growing quickly, it's too easy to not spend time institutionalizing roles and procedures and then when a key employee leaves, you feel the impact far more deeply than you expect.

Also rotate senior managers periodically. People who have these jobs for a long time run them like fiefdoms and don't always look for new solutions or ways to cut costs or improve efficiencies. Most entrepreneurs stay close to their customers. Be sure that key customers have relationships with more than one salesperson on your team. Otherwise, you may risk that customer's business if your key salesperson leaves. Worse, your salesperson may try to take the customer. Confidentiality agreements are essential and are covered later in the Legal section.

Management Tips

This section includes some lessons and tips that are worth remembering as you navigate the bumps in the road.

Complement, Don't Duplicate

Many entrepreneurs don't take the time early on to figure out where their personal knowledge or skills gap are. They're too busy doing a little of everything and don't accurately assess their strengths and weaknesses. With too much to do and anxious to delegate some of their work, entrepreneurs tend to hire people who look like them on paper, thereby duplicating skills and knowledge. Take the time to figure out what you don't know or aren't very good at. Hire to complement your skills and knowledge gaps. If you're great in sales and marketing but aren't as good with numbers, plan to hire a strong financial manager as soon as possible, perhaps even before you staff all of your sales and marketing functions. You'll probably continue to perform the tasks you're good at for several years in your company's growth.

Taking the Unpopular but Needed Action

It's common knowledge that managers sometimes have to make unpopular decisions. As you grow into your managerial role, you must be prepared to do the same. You must be prepared to find yourself the target of displaced anger, hostility, and accusations—sometimes these are deserved, but more often they are not. Accept that you're growing a business, not competing in a popularity contest.

Having character is doing what is right when no one else is looking. Do what you think is right, even if it's not popular. In hard times, make sacrifices before you require them of others. No one likes a pay cut or delayed paycheck, but they can be slightly more bearable if your employees know that you are feeling the pain first. And be sure that if you share the pain during tough times, you also spread the gain during good times.

During bumpy economic times, you may find that you need to downsize. Communicate frequently with your employees through company or group meetings. People often know that times are tough, so layoffs don't always come as a surprise, although it's always painful for an employee to be out of a job.

If your firm can afford to pay severance, it will always be well appreciated, but the reality is that there are no hard-and-fast rules. Some firms give a week for each year worked, others give a month per year of work, while still others who have limited resources give whatever they can. At a minimum, your company should make sure employees have the option of continuing any benefits you offer under Consolidated Omnibus Budget Reconciliation Act (COBRA). This allows them the chance to purchase the same medical and dental benefits for up to 18 months. At most, you'll have a small administrative role but will not incur any medical or dental expense. Discuss the unemployment options your downsized employees can receive with your accountant.

It's important to have some business logic behind your decision of whom to layoff. You may have some legal challenges if you arbitrarily pick some people and not others. You may pick the weakest performers, as documented in the most recent performance review. Realize that people may raise eyebrows if all the downsized employees are of a single race, gender, or age. If you need to, get the input of an HR advisor or your lawyer. Many lawyers will suggest that you ask each downsized employee to sign a release waiving any rights to sue you in the future in exchange for whatever severance or benefits you have agreed to.

Address Rumors Quickly

Rumors spread quickly and distract employees when the company is most in need of their best efforts. Hold weekly meetings at which employees can learn about the difficulties the company faces. Make it clear that there's no place for rumors and that professionalism is expected at all times. While this certainly won't stop the rumors, it helps to set a professional tone. If rumors continue to be circulated by one or a few individuals, you may want to meet with them to address their unprofessionalism. You may also want to discuss their satisfaction with their job and their aspirations within the company. Make it clear that those who succeed will be those with positive, productive, and professional attitudes.

Lastly, set an example. Don't gossip or create rumors. Have a zero tolerance policy on this from day one. If your employees realize that they can't win your favor with juicy gossip, you'll help set a professional standard.

Hire Well, Fire Quickly

Hire well, fire quickly. This is easier said than done. There's probably not a single manager, let alone an entrepreneur, who has not at some point lamented the challenges of identifying and retaining the best candidates. Many entrepreneurs fire too slowly, concerned about any number of factors: loss of productivity or institutional knowledge, personal friendship with the employee, legal reasons, or simply concern over their ability to replace a person or skill set without losing critical time and revenues.

If someone's performance has been lagging or if it never made it to par, meet with him or her at regular intervals for at least a period of 1 to 6 months. Help him or her improve by outlining clear objectives. However, if the employee continues to perform poorly, be quick to let the employee go.

You may also find that despite your best management efforts, some employees are simply negative and will spread their negativity to others in the office. Young companies are small, and people work in close quarters. Get rid of bad apples quickly, as they are certain to create a bad working environment for other employees. Despite what you might think, the other employees are likely to be grateful for your decisive action. Don't hire till you've gotten rid of all the negative energy.

In the steps of the hiring and firing processes, you should work toward creating a positive work environment where employees feel valued and motivated.

If morale has been low for a while, you may consider bringing in an outside business coach to help you or your team members or both. If turnover and morale have been low for a while and they're not related to the outside economic environment, be ready to honestly assess your own management style. A business coach may be able to help you improve your management and communication styles.

Don't Get Isolated

A challenge for entrepreneurial managers is discovering how and when to interact with others in their company. In large companies, corporate executives are physically insulated from day-to-day interactions with their employees and so are shielded from suggestions, criticisms, and even ideas. They're usually on a different floor or area from others and don't always hear everything. They also tend to be physically situated around people who are likely to have the same frame of reference they do.

As you grow, don't let yourself get isolated. Encourage people to keep coming into your office to chat with you; to tell you their honest opinions; and to hear about how products, sales, and processes are progressing. While you are probably busy, it's important to find time for informal information exchanges.

Stay in touch with all parts of your business. The early stages of the business are usually very taxing on entrepreneurs. By the time you can hire experienced managers to spread the workload, you may feel anxious about handing over work. Delegate; don't abdicate. Stay involved and know what is going on in each area of your business. This doesn't mean that you should micromanage. However, you should have a good sense of the workflow.

Additionally, as you enjoy your company's growth phase, don't get too caught up in your success. Stay in touch with the most common elements of your business and remember what helped get you where you are. Don't buy into your good or bad press. Keep in touch with employees, customers, colleagues, and investors. Keep talking to just about anyone who has an opinion or comment on your business, product, or market. Everything is worth listening to at least once—you never know what new opportunities you may uncover.

The Buck Stops Here

Many people don't pay enough attention to the spiritual side of entrepreneurship. Entrepreneurship is a constant soul-searching exercise. When you're not at the top of a corporation or organization, it's much easier to find a scapegoat to blame for any business shortcomings. However, as the founder of your company, you bear full responsibility. As your company grows and experiences the peaks and valleys most young companies experience, be ready to take on all tasks and accept responsibility. Your attitude will guide your team by example.

Recognize and Accept Differences

Give 10 people the same problem and you're likely to have 10 different solutions. Even if the solutions seem similar on the surface, the execution and tone will differ. Managing can really make you realize the extent to which this is true. We're all unique individuals, and we respond differently, guided by any number of factors including our personality, our upbringing, our experiences, and our perspectives. This applies to entrepreneurs, managers, and employees alike. Recognize that you'll need to manage based on an appreciation of different peoples' unique skills, strengths, and challenges.

Learning to Trust Your Business Instinct

Don't get intimidated by competitors, investors, or customers. Trust your instinct and have faith in your ability to listen, analyze, and learn.

We all know that moderate, sustained growth is preferable to explosive growth. Growth that's too fast or too slow is probably not the healthiest, although both kinds of growth can still lead to success in the long run. The pace of growth differs for each type of business and depends on you as well. You need to trust your instincts and also be clear on your personal philosophy; both will help you determine the right pace for your company, market, and timing. It's certainly helpful to have input from seasoned, experienced, and knowledgeable professionals, but at the end of the day, you'll have to learn to trust your own judgment and your own sense of business goals.

Make an effort to lift your head above the daily grind and sniff for new opportunities. Think boldly and be willing to constantly reinvent.

Join or Form a Network or Peer Group

Many entrepreneurs face a feeling of aloneness. There's a limit to what an entrepreneur can share with employees, and while friends and family may mean well, they don't necessarily understand the multiple hats and roles you play or what it really takes to grow a young company. Also, in the early years, most entrepreneurs do not know other entrepreneurs or have trusted and experienced confidantes.

There are two basic types of groups that many entrepreneurs find useful. The first is the more common: networking groups that focus on businesses' needs. The second is peer mentoring networks that focus on the entrepreneur's unique position as owner and executive.

Formal and informal peer mentoring is becoming more common as entrepreneurs seek out others who have successfully steered young and growing companies through start-up phases and growing years. Entrepreneurial support groups function like business peer mentoring where you can freely discuss and exchange issues and receive experienced input from other entrepreneurs. Peer groups are invaluable places to discuss and exchange ideas on managing growing companies as well as obtain introductions to advisors, customers, and possibly investors or venture capitalists.

Networking groups tend to be organized by industry, geography, and type of company. You need to be practical about how many organizations you can join. It's not a productive use of your time to spread yourself too thin. Consider joining a couple of networking groups and one or possibly two peer mentoring groups.

Some of the more popular peer groups for entrepreneurs are the Entrepreneurs' Organization (EO), which consists of Young Entrepreneurs' Organization/World Entrepreneurs' Organization (YEO/WEO), and Young Presidents' Organization (YPO). To join YEO, you need to have $1 million in sales and be under 40 years of age. WEO is the "graduate" level of the organization. Members can join WEO between the ages of 40 and 46 and remain members for life. YPO membership requires members to join prior to their 45th birthday and to meet a number of business requirements that are listed on their Web site at www.ypo .org.

Both organizations have chapters in almost every major city in the United States and around the world. While they are technically different organizations, they work closely together and many entrepreneurs move from YEO to YPO as they become eligible. One of the more valuable parts of these organizations is what they both refer to as the "forum."

Every YEO/WEO/YPO member has the opportunity to join a forum group. The groups meet monthly for a couple of hours and entrepreneurs have the opportunity to discuss a personal or professional issue that is pressing for them, their company, or both. In essence, as the YPO Web site (www.ypo.org/network.html) notes, these forums provide a "safe haven where young leaders faced with similar personal and professional challenges gather to share experiences and consult each other in absolute confidence." These groups provide a unique opportunity for peer mentoring and networking. While the value of your particular forum can depend on group dynamics and the individual participants, many entrepreneurs who join these organizations find forums to be invaluable and one of the key motivators of membership.

Some entrepreneurs prefer to create their own informal peer mentoring group based on factors like compatibility, personal interests, or geographic proximity. For example, some women find that many of the other peer groups have predominantly male members, and as a result, most of the issues discussed tend to exclude work, family, and personal issues that are often experienced by women entrepreneurs, such as pregnancy and the need to take time off or bringing babies to work.

As a result, some women have formed formal and informal peer mentoring groups to exchange information on their diverse entrepreneurial businesses, customers, management issues, and personal lives. Some of the formal groups for women entrepreneurs are the Women Presidents' Organization (WPO), the Committee of 200 (also known as C200), and the National Association of Women Business Owners (NAWBO). The informal groups are often very local and get started by friends and colleagues. Whether you prefer formal or informal groups, make an effort to make them a part of your regular schedule. Even if you just meet monthly for dinner, you have an opportunity to discuss issues, learn new strategies, and get critical advice.

With all the groups, you need to determine what you're looking for. Some provide industry insight, and others are general business peer groups. Some of the organizations are open to membership from entrepreneurs who founded their companies as well as to people who have inherited family run firms or who are senior executives at large companies. Clearly this combination results in a range of issues and focuses. If you're looking for a group of fellow entrepreneurs, then be sure to check the background of others in your peer group. For example, at the YPO level, there's a mix of people with ownership or executive responsibility. As a result, you may be more focused on growth issues and on developing your senior team, whereas a fellow senior executive may be more interested in understanding how to deal with his or her president or board. Further, some of these corporate professionals may have ascended quickly without working in all the roles that you, the entrepreneur, have likely had. In a productive scenario, you'd both learn from each other's perspectives, but you should recognize that each peer group may have a slightly different viewpoint.

Industry groups provide a great opportunity to get to know your competition on neutral turf. These groups serve as networking opportunities rather than as peer exchanges and are likely to be your best source of information. Seek out your competition's executives and get to know them informally. You may want to hire them one day as you grow. Use industry groups as a way to scout out other talent as well.

Finance

Assessing Progress

Most entrepreneurs will tell you there are some "magic milestones" that, when achieved, will improve your company's long-term viability. These often include achieving $2 to $3 million in sales, having at least 5 to 10 employees, and making it past the 3-year mark. These milestones are impacted by your industry and market. It's more important to focus on profitability than on the number of people you employ, and knowing your company's profitability per employee can be very useful. Identify which benchmarks are valuable for your company.

There's also a certain amount of education that comes with early bootstrapping. Even as you grow and have more disposable income, try to not rush to throw money at either opportunities or problems. Analyze and strategize with your team for creative solutions.

Also, as you grow, continue to review what processes you can outsource. The fact that your revenues are increasing does not mean that your expenses need to increase as well. Not all functions need to be performed in-house. For example, it's common in today's world to outsource payroll and other HR functions.

Cash Flow Challenges: Yours and Your Customers'

Just about every entrepreneur has spent a sleepless night or more worrying about his or her ability to make payroll and payables.

Even companies that are doing well and experiencing increasing sales face these issues. Often, when companies grow rapidly, their expenses also grow quickly, and the need for cash increases. Entrepreneurs tend to focus more on sales than on cash. As a result, they're caught short when payments from customers take longer than expected and employees and bills need to be paid. Focus on cash and know your daily cash position. We have done daily cash reconciliation in all of my companies. Further, we do a cash budget alongside any other financial projection. This tells us exactly how much is coming in per month and what is needed to cover expenses for the same month, without tapping reserves. This way we can anticipate shortfalls and incentivize customers to place more orders and make payments more quickly.

Cash flow and profitability should drive your financial analysis more than revenues alone. Sure, you need to increase sales, but if you're not making money and your cash flow is poor, you'll face far more troubles and more quickly than you're likely to anticipate.

When cash flow gets poor, companies often slow down the pace at which they pay bills. Don't just avoid your vendors or ignore bills. Communicate with vendors if payment cycles change. Not all will be willing to work with you, but those that are will deserve your long-term loyalty. If you need to wait until your customer pays you before you can pay certain related expenses, let the vendors know. Again, most will work with your firm in the hopes of increasing long-term opportunities.

Another way to manage your cash flow cycles is to have a standby line of credit to dip into during critical months. If you find that you are using this line monthly, then you may need to determine if you are absorbing this cost or if it is being passed onto your customers. You may also want to consider giving your larger customers incentives like preferential pricing or discounts to pay faster. Ideally, you want to get to a point where you have at least one or more years of expenses in liquid reserves, not including the company's fixed or investment assets or your personal assets. Remember that as you grow, so will your expenses and the amount needed for your annual reserve. Some firms may opt to use a factor or accounts receivable firm as an alternative short-term financing tool. Keep in mind that all these options have a cost. The best option is to strive toward building your company's own reserve.

If your business takes a severe and sustained downturn, acknowledge it as soon as you can. Know your financial and legal options at every stage. Being prepared and knowledgeable will help you avoid nasty surprises. Many companies have to restructure at some time in their corporate histories, even including Chapter 11 reorganization. Doing so earlier rather than later will help you rebuild your company. Neither bankruptcy law nor your customers and vendors will let you restructure often, so make sure to plan carefully and get good legal advice.

Your Customers

Similarly, take a look at your inflow to see if your accounts receivables are taking longer to collect. It's always wise to be in touch with your customers quickly if you detect any changes in their payment cycles. You should monitor your key customers regularly and monitor changes like restructurings, layoffs, mergers, acquisitions, new debt, or equity offerings, all of which could impact payment cycles.

In the interest of building good customer relationships, you should make every effort to work with your clients through any challenging periods. They are likely to be grateful and to perhaps give you more business when their circumstances improve. However, if your customers stop paying, are nonresponsive to your efforts to work with them, or appear to be ready to close or file for bankruptcy, consider using a collection agency as soon as possible.

Your accountant or banker may be able to suggest collection agencies. Some law firms do this as a service. Determine how difficult the collections will be before using a law firm, as law firms tend to cost more. Also, shop around for the most reliable and least expensive option. Make sure that you hire a professional and reputable agency. There are very strict laws governing what and how companies can collect from customers. You don't want to be accused of harassment because your collection agency uses questionable tactics.

In a worst-case scenario, the quicker your efforts, the more likely you'll be to collect even a fraction of what's owed. You should note that if a company does file for Chapter 7 or 11 bankruptcy protection, any payments it makes in the 90 days prior to the filing may need to be returned to the courts. Usually this occurs if the bankruptcy trustee determines that certain creditors received preferential treatment and were paid ahead of other creditors. You'll be advised if this is the case. Just don't be surprised. Additionally, if a customer files, note that you are not allowed to contact them regarding any outstanding invoices.

Getting Robbed

Being cheated by your bookkeeper or accountant is more common than you think. Embezzlement is unfortunately a common occurrence in many young entrepreneurial companies, which often have insufficient controls, despite their best efforts. It's not enough to say that you will be the only signatory on checks, as check forgery is a common form of embezzlement. In addition to being the only signer on accounts, have an independent outside accountant do the monthly bank reconciliations, or at a minimum, do them yourself. It's probably the best way you'll find missing checks that may never have been entered into the accounting system.

A good accountant or finance manager should be able to help you set up critical systems and processes. Consider establishing at least two bank accounts: one for deposits and one to write checks from. This will limit access to the deposit account where you should have more of your money. Transfer money to your checking account weekly to cover payables. Also, keep sizable funds in investment accounts and diversify your banking relationships. You'll be able to determine which of your relationships will provide you with the best and most cost-effective services as you grow. Most banks will waive or adjust your fees when they review the combined relationship. Get to your know your branch manager so that you can identify your options.

It's not just your finances that risk robbery. Equipment, products, and supplies can also be taken by employees or outsiders. Establish procedures early on for things like who can order supplies or equipment. Also, limit access to inventory areas, and depending on your industry, do periodic reconciliations.

Contingency Plans

Contingency plans are essential. You should plan for a range of possible outcomes, including the worst-case scenario. Everything that can go wrong with your business probably will at some point or another.

Contingency plans are not limited to managing through a systems crash, although that is one possible hurdle and is covered in this section. Contingency planning refers in its broadest sense to thinking about what might go wrong or just differently than anticipated and then planning for it to the best of your ability.

For example, what if your major customer, who represents 40% of your revenues, files for bankruptcy? Your contingency plan will need to address how and under what conditions you might still sell to them. You will need to figure out how to find new customers to replace any lost revenue. Your plan will also need to assess how and when you may need to cut staff and expenses to stem any losses. Ideally, you will have already been working on getting new customers long before the crisis, as your business should never be dependent on just one or two major customers. Diversifying your customer base is essential to long-term survival, but it can take time to achieve.

Systems do crash, and you need to plan for this possibility. Young companies with tight budgets often don't have back up systems or off-site data recovery. You need to determine how critical your systems are to your business and prioritize accordingly. If your systems are a core part of your product or service, you may want to consider having your network backed up daily or weekly on-site. If you can also back up critical information remotely or on the Web, you can then have an additional backup in case something happens to your office. Increasingly, companies of all sizes are using cloud computing as an effective way to access business applications online, particularly those providing sales management or HR services. Even if you use online business applications, you'll still need to back up your data. For critical data, it's best to have backups in the office as well as to utilize one of the many online backup service providers.

If you hire systems people, strategize with them on the most cost-effective solution for a backup. If you do not have these skills in-house, consider hiring a systems consultant to help. Of course, these companies are trying to sell you the system, so ask more than one for an opinion. Keep in mind that their business is selling systems and that their suggestions will be far from complete. If your core product or service does not rely on technology, you may only need good systems for backing up sales and finance records.

It's also important to note that contingency planning doesn't always imply planning for a negative scenario. You also need to plan for unseen windfalls or for outcomes that exceed your expectations. For example, you will probably want to plan under what business conditions you would need to hire another sales account manager or more product development people. Sometimes if you get a new piece of business quickly, you may not have enough time to search for the right hires. Planning ahead and keeping a database of potentially qualified people can help you manage in times of sudden growth. Contingency plans help you identify which variables can impact your business, positively or negatively.

Legal

All young companies encounter a range of standard legal issues as they grow. Protecting your business, products, and know-how is essential. Additionally, almost all companies get sued at some point. Understand how these legal scenarios can impact your business.

Protecting Your Intellectual Property and Confidentiality

It's important to protect your intellectual property (IP) and confidential information. In addition to filing for patents as applicable and registering trademarks and copyrights, you need to protect your intellectual property from full-time and part-time employees, consultants, investors, board and advisory members, as well as anyone else to whom you disclose information. Your confidentiality agreement is separate from any employment offer, contract, or retainer agreement. The latter two may include a confidentiality clause. Many institutional sales and distribution agreements include a confidentiality clause along with noncompete clauses. Make noncompete provisions standard in all of your agreements, although their term and scope may differ. More senior employees definitely need a noncompete clause that extends a couple of years beyond their involvement with your company. You may want to consider providing a formula for the penalty so that if someone does breach this provision, you do not have to spend an enormous amount of money to prove how much your business suffered.

Most lawyers have templates of these agreements that can be customized for your company quickly and cheaply. You need to protect your company, especially when competitors try to poach your sales, marketing, and product teams. In your agreement, it's important to clearly state that "confidential" information includes everything about your product, customers, business model, and company know-how. While this may seem overly legal, a good definition actually protects you by being comprehensive. There are many variations, and your lawyer can help customize a definition that best suits your company, market, and recipient.

An agreement won't prevent an employee from trying to take customers, but it may dissuade them if they understand that you intend to pursue legal action if they try. The more thorough your legal agreements, the better your ability to dissuade.

In addition to using agreements, many companies seek to limit employee and consultant access to different types of information, including customer databases, product specifications, and pricing models. For example, some companies simply restrict computer access. Today's office networks make this relatively easy to accomplish. It's best to protect your IP with a combination of legal documents and daily operational processes.

Getting Sued

Almost all businesses are likely to get sued at some point, rightly or wrongly accused of a business, personnel, or related infringement. For many first-time entrepreneurs, this can come as a shock. Most people never encounter the legal system on a personal level. In large companies, legal issues are dealt with separately from the business, and as a result, most employees are not even aware of these occurrences.

Get good and appropriate counsel. Make sure your lawyer has experience in the area of law you need. For example, get a labor lawyer if an employee is suing you. Get a good intellectual property lawyer if your product patent or trademark is being challenged by another company. Most importantly, don't take the suit personally. Law suits are just a part of business. Focus on responding professionally and consistently, particularly if you are being sued by an employee.

Issues With Investors, Venture Capitalists (VCs), and Partners Building Trust

As you navigate bumps in the road and experience growth, you'll find that some bigger and more complex decisions would benefit not just from the input of experts but also from the input of trusted confidantes. Good confidantes are people who have experienced many growth challenges and opportunities in your industry, with whom you can share details of the company's financial and market status. For some people, this may be one or more members of their board or advisory council; for some, it may include their company's senior managers; and for others, it may be a business consultant or fellow entrepreneur. Just be sure that you understand your confidante's varying motivations, strengths, and weaknesses.

One of my institutional investors potentially fit the category of a good confidante. As an astute and seasoned owner and manager of profitable businesses, he had some critical and valuable experiences that would have helped me navigate some entrepreneurial bumps in the road. However, his previous professional (and personal) dealings with my other institutional investors complicated the company dynamics, and their mutual mistrust made his advice suspect, even when it was sound. I resolved the situation by looking outside and bringing in a senior and experienced advisor, who became a reliable and trusted business confidante. Knowing who to trust can be challenging, but it's essential to nurture your own small team of business confidantes.

Reassessing Your Role

As your company grows, you'll need to transition from an entrepreneur who is involved in doing everything to more of a strategic role. As we all know, the role of a CEO in a start-up and growth phase is different than the same role in a larger, established company. You'll need to honestly ask yourself if you are willing and able to make that transition. If you have outside VC capital and a board, they may very well be asking the same questions. By addressing the issue proactively, you can determine the roles you want to take on and are best suited for. You can then develop a senior team to complement your position and role. For example, if you're a creative person who enjoys being close to the product or service and the customer, you may want to be the CEO and head of creative. You can then search for a competent chief operating officer (COO) to run the company's operations.

Managing Issues With Partners

If you're in a partnership, at some point you'll encounter issues with your partner. Even if you have a partnership agreement, it's the day-to-day issues that can make partnerships frustrating as well as rewarding. While it's useful to share responsibilities and workloads, many entrepreneurs don't clarify roles until conflicts arise. The more successful partnerships iron out responsibilities and clarify roles early on and acknowledge that these roles may need to evolve as the company grows.

There are also many partners who do not enter into partnership agreements when they first start their companies. Years later, they may recognize the need for an agreement, but the stresses of running the company together may make it harder to agree on critical points such as exit strategies and valuing the company. If you have not had the time to create an agreement, aim to address this problem within the coming year. If your company has grown significantly, you'll both probably need lawyers to ensure that the full range of issues is adequately and fairly addressed. This is also a good way to put the agreement on a schedule, though, of course, if you can't reach consensus, no amount of scheduling will produce an agreement.

Aside from agreements, there may be differences in how you see the organization and its future. If neither of you wants to exit the company, you may want to consider splitting the business in two, with each of you heading one part. It may be better to divide the company by product lines or markets as customers can come and go. Some partners actually start new related businesses in an effort to address management and control issues. This strategy simply allows you to continue operating. At some point though, you will still need to address how you can both exit the business. However, if you both are running successful related businesses, there's a better chance of reaching an agreement on your combined holdings.

Some partners hire business consultants to come in and assess the partners or team for strengths and weaknesses in an effort to determine the company's best structure. Ask other partnerships how they have addressed their issues. They'll probably have some good suggestions and perhaps referrals for business consultants and coaches.

Delaying or Deferring Your Compensation

You may opt or be asked to defer your compensation for a short or extended period of time. Doing so for several months may be in the best interests of the company. However, even if you can handle a deferment, think carefully about doing so if it's a condition of your investors, particularly if they have sale, merger, or liquidation preferences over you. What are they really asking you to do? If you have external investors, it's important to realize that your rights are different than if you owned the company outright. You should consider protecting your interests by negotiating your willingness to defer compensation. You may want to ask for additional equity or a cash bonus once the company's performance improves. Any conditions should be documented to protect your interests. If you own your company 100%, then your ability to repay yourself in later months or years is completely your decision, although you should review any tax consequences with your accountant.

Having said that, many entrepreneurs defer compensation for one or more months, sometimes even a year, to help their companies get through challenging periods. Always be sure you have incurred the "pain" of deferred compensation before passing it on to others on your team.

Growth

Planning as You Expand

As you expand and grow, planning continues to revolve around three basic questions:

1. What is the new unique opportunity? It may be a new product version or new market.
2. Who is going to tackle the new opportunity? Do you have the team in place? How quickly can you hire?
3. Do you have what you need to engage the new challenge in terms of other resources?

Each of these core questions requires attention to details. Entrepreneurs occasionally get caught up in the lingo. Every industry, including entrepreneurship, has lingoes and cultures uniquely its own. Don't get caught up in the lingo. Focus on the underlying concepts and opportunities.

For every new product or market extension, you should plan to develop a mini business plan complete with financial projections. You should treat these new opportunities as their own separate profit and loss center. This will enable you to measure success, and if your new venture doesn't work out, it will help you decide how soon to pull the plug.

Even as you experience fast growth, you don't need all your resources immediately. Focus on achievable short-term, monthly, or quarterly goals so you can assess progress and continuously adjust your planning.

Growth Through Acquisition

Many young companies grow by acquiring other firms. We read about high-profile, large acquisitions every day. In reality, there are many more small acquisitions that occur routinely and give growing companies faster access to products, markets, and customers.

If you're a young company, it's likely that you will know who you want to buy based on your own industry research and knowledge. You may have also gotten to know the other business owner through the industry, and he or she may have approached you, offering their company for sale. Take your time and do a full legal and financial due diligence. Also check to see if you have compatible and complementary businesses in terms of products, services, employees, culture, and operational style. Before you finalize an acquisition, it's very helpful to complete a full business plan for the new company. In preparing the plan, you'll be able to identify any weak areas and address them. Even just being aware of the weaknesses will help avoid nasty surprises postacquisition.

One of the critical issues is the ongoing role, if any, of the other company's senior executives and, if applicable, entrepreneurs. Before you decide who stays and who doesn't, you may want to hire a business consultant to help do a team assessment of capabilities, strengths, and weaknesses. You'll need to address ways to integrate the work teams from both companies so they all feel essential to the company's growth and clearly understand the company's vision and mission. All the other company's team should sign new confidentiality and noncompete agreements with your firm.

Growth Through an Initial Public Offering

For some entrepreneurs, going public through an initial public offering (IPO) provides a financial exit strategy from which they can cash out some of their gains. However, for most entrepreneurs, the IPO is more of a financing strategy through which they can fund expansion as well as reap some financial benefits from what's likely to have been years of hard work. There are limits to how much money an entrepreneur can take out in an IPO. For one thing, it may imply low confidence in the business if you sell a majority of your stock in the days after going public, just when you're asking others to invest in the company. In most situations, the entrepreneur is limited in how much stock he or she can sell over the course of 1 to 2 years.

Regardless of which exchange you go public on, you need to plan for at least around $1 million in expenses, including investment banking and legal fees as well as those for marketing, administrative, and investor or public relations (PR) firms. The expense increases with the amount of your IPO.

To complete an IPO, you will need an investment bank. Your best bet is to start by asking for referrals from lawyers and accountants. You'll want all of your advisors to have completed successful initial public offerings, and you may need to switch lawyers or hire a new additional team to complete this growth strategy. You'll also need a PR or investor relations firm that has experience in communicating effectively with shareholders and analysts. Some young companies that go public outsource the shareholder relations for several years until it makes sense to hire an in-house person.

As you go through the IPO process, you should remember a few things. First, you are likely to be distracted by the fundraising process, which includes meetings and the actual road show, when you travel to meet with prospective shareholders and analysts to encourage them to purchase your stock as well as view it favorably. Post IPO, you'll also spend a great deal of time communicating with these stakeholders.

Further, if you are going to go public in the next few years of your company's growth, consider spreading the potential gain, establishing an options plan, or giving stock as an incentive. This will motivate everyone toward the IPO goal. Once you have gone public, and if it's successful, you may have to think about how you are going to retain your employees. Fostering a good work environment will help stem any employee losses in the post-IPO world. While you are preparing to go public, consider hiring an HR consultant to specifically address the impact on employees and the resulting impact on the company. You'll need to think about how to keep employees focused and productive as well as address disparities among people who benefited more than others from an IPO. Develop a plan for retaining and motivating post-IPO employees, although if it's very successful, you're bound to lose some who now have the financial freedom to pursue different personal dreams.

Tales From the Trenches

Rosalind Resnick built her Internet marketing company, NetCreations, Inc., from a two-person home-based start-up to a public company in just 5 years. She cofounded NetCreations by pioneering opt-in e-mail marketing. Unlike many of its competitors, NetCreations generated *both* revenues and profits. Resnick initially resisted pressures to raise capital, but eventually she saw going public as a way to expand as well as harness some of the company's value in the strong public markets.

Further, with so many of her competitors raising capital through VCs or through the public markets, Resnick and her partner had few options if they wanted to remain a leader in their market. They also wanted to retain management control of their business and preferred to go public instead of being acquired. Resnick and her partner made their final decision to go public when their biggest reseller raised significant VC money and became their biggest competitor almost overnight.

At the start of their efforts, Resnick and her partner were turned down by every New York investment bank, all of whom saw them as too small and lacking in critical VC support, which was considered essential at the time. In the end, they chose a smaller boutique investment bank, Friedman Billings Ramsey (FBR), because the firm was smaller and "hungrier" for the business.

As is typical for IPO companies, their road show lasted 3 weeks. They visited 13 cities and had 71 meetings. The company successfully went public, reaching the astronomical heights that were standard for the dotcom boom. On the first day of trading, they had a market capitalization of $300 million, and 3 months later it was almost $1 billion.

More telling, though, are Resnick's personal observations about running a public company, which she equates with doing business in a fishbowl with a gun pointed at your head. Managing employee, investor, and public expectations can be very demanding, as there's a constant expectation that CEOs and their team can somehow predict the future. There's no room for error in earnings predictions and forecasts, and the company is inevitably forced to think very short-term.

For Resnick, going public is only a strategy; not the end game. There are other ways to raise money, expand your company, compete with other larger companies in your market, and, of course, cash out value from your firm. More than a year after going public, Resnick and her partner accepted a generous offer to buy NetCreations.

Successfully navigating the entrepreneurial bumps in the road and taking advantage of market timing proved a financial boon for Resnick and her partner. They walked away from the IPO and acquisition ready to start their next venture—with their own money.

Changing Directions

It's very possible that, despite your best efforts, something in the market, the product, or the timing didn't fit. It may be that while your company is profitable, you don't have significant growth or see long-term opportunities within your current business model or product line. Should this be the case, you don't necessarily need to close the company. Instead, you can opt to change directions. This is one clear reason many successful entrepreneurs say it's a good idea to focus on creating a company, not just a product or service.

Usually the hardest thing about changing directions is, quite frankly, attitude: yours and that of your team. We all get set in our ways, and it's even tougher to challenge our assumptions when business looks OK or even good. But every type of business has to challenge its foundation and business model in order to survive the long-term. Even more successful and established companies challenge their assumptions about their market and business models.

In an ideal world, you would have time to plan a new product or new direction without having to meet other obligations. In the real world, you'll have to plan while you are running your business in its current form. Time will be limited, as resources and even your energy has its bounds. One way is to take a day or a half day every week to focus on researching new strategies, markets, and products. In essence, you are creating a new business plan and may even need to test a few assumptions before you finalize. For example, you may think you sense a new market, but you'll need to gather research and talk to potential customers. You may even need to build a demo product to test customer interest. Likewise, it can be difficult to change business models when your customers have certain expectations and when the pricing models of your industry are well entrenched.

The key is to stay open and flexible and to be willing to challenge your own assumptions. Focus on your company's survival, not that of a favorite product or service. Be willing to reinvent your entire approach, including your products and services as well as your business model and strategy.

CHAPTER 4

Keeping the Faith

Okay, for some this chapter may seem corny, simplistic, or filled with clichés, but the reality is that every entrepreneur goes through ups and downs. Finding ways to keep the faith is essential to your company and to your personal long-term survival. By faith, I am not referring to religion, although for many that may certainly be an essential component. How you keep your faith is tied more to your personal and managerial philosophy. It will shape how you deal with problems, people, and challenges. Entrepreneurship is certainly not for the faint of heart. You need to determine before you get into it if you have the stomach for the often rapid ups and downs. The more you talk to fellow entrepreneurs, the more you'll see that just about everyone has their own ways of keeping the faith and moving forward during challenging times. This chapter highlights many ways that people keep the faith, professionally and personally. During your entrepreneurial ride, it's important to keep an eye on both your spiritual and physical health.

In essence, there are two distinct scenarios in which your entrepreneurial faith may feel challenged. The first occurs during the normal course of starting and growing your company and is related to the problems, issues, and challenges that just about every company faces. Even when you know you're not alone in confronting these problems, keeping focused, committed, and positive takes effort.

The second is the unfortunate but very common scenario of closing your business. In this chapter, I'll focus on how to move past closing your company to the next step. Successful career entrepreneurs learn from their failures, and closing one company doesn't mean you won't be successful with the next. Learning how to keep the faith will help you in both scenarios.

It Happens to Everyone

The first thing to realize is that everyone, including entrepreneurs, experiences challenges and makes mistakes. The key is to learn from them. In fact, many professionals find that their challenges, mistakes, and hardships help them find future successes. So the key to keeping faith is figuring out how to go through the fire of challenge and emerge scathed but not destroyed, ready to move toward the next opportunity.

Failure is a part of life for just about everyone. What starts to differentiate people is our ability to respond to failure—our degree of resilience. Whether it's a politician with one or more previous election losses who keeps the faith and comes back to win an election, an actor who endures a pile of rejections before getting a prized part, an athlete who never gives up hope of being number one, or a career entrepreneur who keeps believing in a vision and comes back to start a successful company, a resilient person remains open to future success. Entrepreneurs need to find ways to cope with adversity and overcome the professional and personal challenges associated with their ventures.

An essential first step is to stop feeling sorry for yourself, determine what went wrong and why, and then move on. It's important to distinguish that it was the company that failed. The entrepreneur as a person is not a failure.

Some Common Reasons a Project, Idea, or Company Stumbles

Not every venture will succeed. Sometimes, the business model isn't right, the product doesn't meet the need, or the market timing is not right. These things can occur for reasons beyond the entrepreneur's control. The following will help you begin to dissect your own experience. Keep in mind that you can't be afraid to make mistakes. If you are, you will most likely hold yourself back in either your current or future ventures.

- *Not enough planning.* Did your plan get enough market input from customers and users? Were the financials thorough or did you underestimate expenses and overestimate the timing of sales?

- *Not enough resources.* Did you have what you needed to execute your plan in terms of people, money, skills, and supplies? Were you able to reach your customer or was the marketing budget too small? Were you capitalized in a way that was productive for your company or that was disincentivizing for you and the other senior team members?

- *External factors (economy, market, or industry not yet ready).* Did you launch in a recession or at the end of an upcycle? Would your product have fared better in a booming economy? Often, for price sensitive, nonessential products, market timing is everything. Did you have enough resources to ride through a tough economic cycle? How could you have planned for it? Did you need to raise VC money in a weak market? Can you put your idea or company on hold for a short while until the market improves? Are you ahead of the market or behind it?

- *Incorrect team.* Did you hire the wrong senior team or did you lack the resources to even have a senior team, forcing you to take on roles that you were not as strong in? Did you duplicate rather than complement your skills? (See chapter 3.)

- *Partnership and ownership disputes and changes.* Did differences in strategy or management direction become irreconcilable? Did one or more partners cease to be involved with the company or did ownership change and the company's prospects take a turn for the worse?

- *Inability to fulfill demand or grow quickly.* Did you actually succeed in getting orders but fail to have enough resources to fulfill them? Products need parts and if you can't buy the parts, you can't make the products to fill the orders. Not having short-term cash to cushion growth is as much a challenge as not having the orders to begin with.

Listen, Analyze, and Learn

Everyone, including employees, colleagues, investors, customers, family, and friends, will undoubtedly have their own opinion about why a product, marketing campaign, or your business failed. It's normal to feel down and to not want to be bothered by others, no matter how well-meaning. But it's important to review scenarios, processes, and decisions. There may be some information that, if processed differently, may have helped you to make different decisions. If you can't examine your mistakes and failures, you're likely to make the same mistakes again.

Having said that, you should avoid listening to people whose criticism is too vehement or worse, too personal to be productive. Amid useful business and market information will likely be nestled a strong dose of unproductive blame, most likely from investors or others who had a vested interest in the business. Block that out. Yes, of course you probably made some errors. Who doesn't? If you accept responsibility and learn from your mistakes, you're likely to operate differently and more likely successfully in the future.

Decisions can be hard to navigate. We make decisions based on information we know at that moment in time, without the benefit of a crystal ball (though wouldn't that be nice?). The information we evaluate comes from inside as well as outside our company. The silver lining in making a mistake is that our leaning process is made easier. We can analyze cause and effect so we're better equipped next time.

For example, imagine a scenario in which, to increase sales in a down economy, a company drops its prices. When the economy improves, the industry and customers won't allow the company to raise them again and as a result, the firm loses revenues and profitability. The next time around, that company will know to think of better ways to generate revenues and won't drop its prices quickly, if at all. That's one example of a lesson that could only come with experience or from a seasoned entrepreneur.

Don't wallow in your errors or misfortunes. If you made a mistake, recognize it and then get on with your life. We all learn more from our mistakes than from our successes. Determine what aspects of your business model or corporate structure didn't work. If you decide to start a new venture, you need to be careful not just to rebuild what you lost but to build with newer and wiser information. If you're unable to truly listen and analyze, you're likely to keep making the same mistakes, no matter how great your idea.

Also, realize that you probably did some things right and that the company had a few successes. Isolate these so you can consider how to use these nuggets of information in your next venture.

Focus on Positivity

Get rid of negativity. If this sounds like a mantra from a new age self-help book, it probably is. However, I have watched it work beautifully, both in my own experiences and in those of many around me.

Corporations spend millions on team-building and coaching, but at the end of the day, it's about being focused and positive. You can't do that if you have one or more people in your world who are negative, particularly if that person is you or someone on your team.

Start with yourself. Are you a glass half-full or a glass half-empty kind of person? Knowing your personal philosophy and your personal temperament can help you understand how you approach stress. Every new and growing venture goes through stressful periods. You need to think about how you respond to stress and if your response is generating the right, positive energy for you and your company.

Negative energy on your team can be disastrous for a young company. I have heard entrepreneurs talk about "flushing" their teams. This may not sound very pleasant, or even very polite, but it refers to "flushing" or letting go of people who are negative and unproductive. "Flushing" is the easiest way to get everyone back on track and moving toward positive growth. Negative people will spread their negativity. In young companies, which are typically still small, bad energy can spread faster than the speed of light.

Now, this does not mean that you should surround yourself with "yes" men and women either. Find people whose experiences, attitudes, and opinions you respect and who complement you, not copy you. You want people who can identify problems and challenges, hopefully before they happen. While positive people are likely to recognize both the problem and its potential solutions, a negative person is likely to dwell on the problem without pushing past it toward a solution.

As part of focusing on positive energies, take a look at the extended network of your family and friends. Some may inadvertently pass their fears onto you. Remember that these fears result more often from their own discomfort with the world of entrepreneurship than from other, more legitimate sources. Beware of negative energies, which may distract you. Once you have heard the message, separate constructive criticisms or projections from the purely negative energy. Remember what's constructive and throw the rest away. If you don't, negative energy will impede your ability to creatively think your way out of tough situations. A positive and open-minded attitude will help you tackle the toughest adversities.

Your Attitude Is Contagious

Your employees will glean a great deal about the company from your attitude and perspective. There's certainly no need to hide the fact that your company may be experiencing challenging times. In fact, quite the opposite is true. Your employees will know about the challenges whether you tell them or not; if you recognize the issues openly, they will more likely respect and appreciate your professionalism, candidness, and leadership.

In stressful periods, it's common to be down or even grumpy. But if you genuinely believe that your firm can turn around, then your employees need to see and hear that energy. If you have resources, you may want to bring in a motivational coach to help find ways to get everyone excited and focused. If it's likely that your company will need to close and you don't have resources, small gestures will go a long way in recognizing an employee's effort. Even during difficult periods, find something positive to note. It might be an employee's work or attitude or a product or new customer.

Letting Go of Anger

As your company goes through a closing, your anger and resentment are likely to increase, particularly if they are directed at a particular person or entity. Of course, you are more likely to assign the blame to someone other than yourself, although some people habitually accept more blame than may be due them. It may seem easy and comforting to be mad at investors, employees, customers, the market, and even family or friends for any variety of reasons, not the least of which is their failure to provide support. It should be no great surprise to hear that left unchecked, anger can be self-defeating.

A truly remarkable story of moving past anger comes from the life of Nelson Mandela, a man who was warranted in feeling more than just a little angry at his jailers. Instead, Mandela realized that if he remained angry, it would be like leaving one kind of imprisonment for another. By letting go of his anger and resentment, he set himself free. Try to find your own inspiration in people who overcome and go on to achieve their visions.

Keeping Perspective

One essential part of keeping the faith is keeping perspective. We get so caught up in the crisis of the moment that we're unable to detach and focus on solutions. We torment ourselves with needless stress. Keeping perspective is essential. I learned this early on. In college, when I would call home stressed about the semester's series of exams, my mother would walk me through a soothing exercise that calculated the number of exams per semester, multiplied by the number of semesters over the 4-year period. Suddenly, when it was one of about 160 exams, the pending test seemed much less stressful.

The lesson here is that you should take any complex and challenging issues and break them into smaller parts that can be handled one by one. Avoid becoming overwhelmed into inaction. Try to break every issue into "bite-size" pieces. Often, it's helpful to work backward when contemplating a particularly difficult problem. Determine the worst-case scenario and work backward to identify solutions.

Don't Take Yourself Too Seriously

By now, it should be clear that all businesses, including entrepreneurial businesses, experience cycles. We've all known plenty of successful, arrogant professionals who were later humbled by life's ups and downs. Stay consistent and stay humble—it will endear you to your employees, customers, and investors alike. As my folks always say, "Be nice to everyone on your way up. You never know when you'll meet them on your way down."

Keep a Sense of Humor and Find Inspiration

Laughter is truly a great medicine. Find ways to bring it into your office, even in the worst of times. Find a Web site that has acceptable jokes or inspirational sayings of the day or week, and pass them through your office. Find ways to laugh at yourself. If you tend to be stiff and proper, your team will likely appreciate the effort even more. You may even break away to see a funny movie or bring one in and have an office video lunch on a Friday. It will help everyone relax. And who knows? Some creative solutions may creep in.

The most important thing to keep in mind is to avoid "hiding." No doubt, you can't see much to laugh about or even to be grateful for. But it's important to lighten the atmosphere of the office. You need people to stick around and be productive, whether you're just going through a prolonged slump or whether you have to close your company. You may find that some people respond better to humor and others to words of inspiration. As a manager, use whichever works best to keep your team energized and focused, no matter which direction your company is headed.

Get a Hobby and a Charitable Interest

Having a balanced personal life will make you a better entrepreneur in any situation. Having a hobby will keep you balanced, and having a charitable interest keeps you humbled and focused on what matters most in the long run. Don't wait until times are tough to develop your interests. As your company grows, having outside personal interests will round out your perspective, keep your outlook positive and keep your ideas fresh and creative. Even with entrepreneurial pressures, it's worth carving out time for personal activities.

If your business stumbles, your family and friends are your likely support and lifeline in the first few months. Having a long-term hobby or charitable interest will continue to give you a sense of purpose and meaning as you regroup and move on to your next venture.

Keeping the Faith in Yourself and in Entrepreneurship

Many entrepreneurs launch and grow several companies before reaching real professional and financial success. Knowing when to move on is a real challenge for most entrepreneurs. After all, our companies are very often extensions of ourselves, children of sorts. It's very difficult for most entrepreneurs to clinically assess when their companies have lived out their useful lives and when termination is best. External confidantes can be very helpful in helping us honestly and accurately assess the moment at which a company must be closed. Pay particular attention to counsel from people who have no vested interest in keeping the company alive. Employees and angel investors have much to lose as well and may also hesitate from making a tough call. Most VCs, on the other hand, are quick to cut their losses, although many are happy if someone else continues to sustain their investment in the slim possibility of a turnaround.

While deciding to close may be one of the hardest steps, it's also one of the most essential skills required. Companies are sometimes kept alive by "artificial measures": through the entrepreneur's passion and resources and possibly through outside funding. You need to focus on why your company is not self-sustaining and how long you should keep it going. Just as strategies need to evolve and move on, sometimes you may need to actually move on from the entire company.

Career entrepreneurs often find that their natural determination and resilience enables them to overcome the bigger bumps in the road.

Closing a Business

Closing a business in our success-obsessed society can be very hard, yet many entrepreneurs are faced with this predicament each year. It's tempting to see the entrepreneurs facing this situation as failures or perhaps quitters. The reality I have observed is that it takes more courage and wisdom to know when to close a business and when and how to do it as best as possible. Accepting the situation, addressing it, and moving on are key to long-term survival and resilience. If you have to close a business, think carefully about who you take along to any subsequent ventures. This includes employees, investors, and advisors. Negative energy is not worth transferring, and you're not obliged to take anyone you don't want to take.

Experiencing the failure of an entrepreneurial venture can feel like the stages of bereavement. The resulting grief can last from a few months to several years, often depending on how personally impacted you are as well as how well you learn to keep the faith and move on. Allow yourself to feel each emotion, such as anger, sadness, and frustration, but don't dwell on them.

In fact, despite the initial pain, going through the closing of your company can actually help you emerge as a stronger and more competent entrepreneur. You have to be willing to analyze your mistakes as well as recognize which factors were beyond your control. The humility and new sense of purpose often makes career entrepreneurs more open to new opportunities.

Optimism and Resilience

Entrepreneurs are an incredibly optimistic lot. We'll always find that one hint of light peeking through even on the dreariest days. Stay focused on that optimism, resilience, and determination. Certainly, don't let it blind you to the real problems, but let it help motivate you to find creative solutions and persevere to your next venture.

Glossary

accounts payable: Often abbreviated as A/P. Accounts payable are the amounts your company owes to vendors. At any given time, it's your company's outstanding, unpaid bills.

accounts receivable: Often abbreviated as A/R. Accounts receivable are the amounts due to your company from customers and other debtors.

accrual method of accounting: Under the accrual method, your company books a sale when you make it, even if the money has not been received. Your company records expenses when you receive the products or services even if you have not paid for them. The other accounting method is the cash method.

asset: Anything of value that your company owns. It can be tangible, like property or equipment, or intangible, such as intellectual property. Assets are noted on the balance sheet.

balance sheet: Shows a picture of your company's assets, liabilities, and equity on a specific date.

capital: Capital is the money invested in the business and is also referred to as equity.

cash flow: Measures cash in and out of a business over a period of time. Positive cash flow means more cash is coming into the business, and negative means the opposite. It's an important barometer of a company's financial health.

cash method of accounting: Under the cash accounting method, revenues and expenses are booked when the monies are received or paid.

collateral: Assets pledged as security for a loan.

control: The shareholder who has majority voting interest in a company.

convertible debt: Debt that has the option, but usually not the obligation, to convert into equity at a certain price and/or under specified conditions.

debt: An obligation of the company to repay a borrowed amount of money.

EBIT: Earnings before interest and taxes.

EBITDA: Earnings before interest, taxes, depreciation, and amortization.

equity: The shares of the company owned by an individual or institutional investor.

first right of refusal: Usually a concept in investor, usually strategic, or partnership agreements. It means that if the company wants to sell itself, the investor or partner has the option to decide whether to buy before it can consider outside offers.

founders stock: The entrepreneur's share given at the time the company is founded.

gross income: The total income or revenues booked by a company during its fiscal period, which usually coincides with a calendar year.

gross profit: The total revenue minus the direct costs of generating that revenue. Gross profit is calculated by the following formula:

$$\text{total revenues (sales)} - \text{cost of goods sold (COGS)} = \text{gross profit}$$

gross profit margin: Also called gross margin or margin, it's a percentage that is calculated by dividing the gross profit by total revenues or sales. The more you pay for supplies or direct labor (the cost of goods sold), the lower the margin. The lower the margin, the less profitable your product or service. The gross profit margin indicates the efficiency of your company. Companies strive to have a higher gross profit margin than their competitors.

Gross profit margin by product is calculated by the following formula:

$$(\text{selling price} - \text{cost}) \div \text{selling price} = \text{gross profit margin}$$

To calculate gross profit margin for your firm, use the following formula:

$$(\text{total revenues} - \text{COGS}) \div \text{total revenues} = \text{gross profit margin}$$

(To state as a percentage, multiply the gross profit margin calculated by the above formulas by 100.)

income statement: A financial statement showing revenues, expenses, and net profits.

inverted balance sheet: A scenario where liabilities exceed assets on a balance sheet.

liabilities: The amounts that a company owes. Liabilities are noted on the balance sheet.

line of credit: A loan that is available as needed by your company for up to a fixed amount and during a certain time period. There's often a small fee to secure the line of credit even if you do not use it. You can access the funds only when you need them and repay them without penalty. There are variations on the terms for a line of credit.

liquidation preferences: The order of priority in which secured and unsecured creditors of a business are paid in the event of a liquidation.

liquidation: When the assets of a business are sold.

long-term loan: A loan that is to be repaid on a term longer than one year.

net income: Net income is the income minus expenses. It's also referred to as net profit.

net worth: Assets minus liabilities is the company's net worth, also referred to as equity.

operating income: Operating income equals revenues minus expenses for cost of goods sold, selling expenses and general and administrative expenses. It does not include any expenses for interest and taxes.

percentage mark-up: The gross profit expressed as a percentage of cost as opposed to margin, which is a percentage of the selling price. Percentage mark-up is calculated by the following formula:

$$(\text{selling price} - \text{cost}) \div \text{cost} \times 100 = \text{percentage mark-up}$$

To calculate gross profit margin by product, please refer to the formula noted in the gross profit margin entry.

preferred stock (equity): A class of stock that usually pays dividends and has a preference over common stock in the payment of dividends and in a liquidation.

revenues: Income from all sources before any deductions are taken.

secured loan: A loan that is guaranteed by collateral that has been pledged as security.

seed capital: Often refers to the initial investment in a company by the entrepreneur, angel investors, and friends and family. The aggregate amount is usually under $1 million.

stock: Refers to ownership in a company.

term loan: A loan that is lent in one or more lump sums and must be repaid according to specified terms. The funds cannot be reborrowed as with a line of credit.

venture capitalist: Often abbreviated as VC. A venture capitalist is an individual who invests in a new or fast-growing company.

Index

www.ingramcontent.com/pod-product-compliance
Lightning Source LLC
Chambersburg PA
CBHW071447200326
41519CB00019B/5651